OREGON COAST RECREATIONAL ATLAS

**A Guide to Natural Resources and Recreational
Opportunities**

by

Timothy J. Sullivan

Maps by

Joseph A. Bernert
and
Sharon M. Murfield-Tyler

E&S Geographic and Information Services, Corvallis, Oregon

OREGON COAST RECREATIONAL ATLAS

A Guide to Natural Resources and Recreational Opportunities

E&S Geographic and Information Services
P.O. Box 609
Corvallis, OR 97339 USA

Cover by John Bennett

Printed in the United States of America

Publisher's Cataloging-in-Publication Data

Sullivan, Timothy J.

    Oregon Coast Recreational Atlas: A Guide to Natural Resources and Recreational Opportunities/by Timothy J. Sullivan; maps by Joseph A. Bernert and Sharon M. Murfield-Tyler

    Includes maps
    Includes bibliographic references
    Includes index

    1. Outdoor recreation - Oregon. 2. Oregon - Description and travel - Guide Books. I Title. II Author.

    GV 199.42 1991 917.95 91-72792

ISBN 1-880062-21-6

TABLE OF CONTENTS

For Debbie, Laura, and Jenna,
with Love

ACKNOWLEDGEMENTS

Many individuals have provided assistance of various kinds in the preparation of the Oregon Coast Recreational Atlas, including designing and constructing the maps, word processing, providing natural resource and recreation information, reviewing draft maps and text, and assisting us in assembling the finances necessary to complete the project. We are very grateful to all who have contributed to this effort.

The series of 24 sectional maps constitute the heart of this atlas. Joe Bernert is mainly responsible for the map design and formatting; without his help and expertise, this atlas would not have been possible. The maps were constructed by Joe and Sharon Murfield-Tyler, with considerable assistance from Dean Tyler and David Fowell. Their efforts are greatly appreciated. Jayne Charles kindly performed all of the word processing and desktop publishing activities. We drove the length of the coast during this project to verify the accuracy of the map presentations. Joe Eilers, Joe Bernert, Debbie Sullivan, Laura Sullivan, and Jenna Sullivan all helped with this effort.

Preparation of this atlas was funded in part with funds from the Oregon State Lottery, through the Regional Strategies Fund administered by the State of Oregon Economic Development Depart-ment. These funds were provided through the Linn-Benton Regional Strategies Business Services Fund and Investment Incentives Fund. The financial package was completed with the benefit of considerable effort on the part of Keith Miller and Cheryl Coate of the Regional Strategy, and also Dennis Sargent, Sheryl Bennett, and Debbie Wright. We gratefully acknowledge their assistance. Thanks also to Mel Chase and Tommy Thompson, Bureau of Land Management, and Jay Rasmussen, Coastal Zone Management Association, for additional assistance.

Helpful suggestions regarding coastal resources were provided by Robin Brown, Roy Lowe, Darrell Demory, Sallie Jacobsen, Peter Bond, Maura Naughton, Monte Turner, Jan Smith, Beverly Vogt, Marty Giles, Reg Pullen, Don Newman, Warren Strycker, Marty Law, Barbara Hutchison, Bill Hastie, Don Byard, Dick Lilja, Jim Barry, and John Phillips.

Review comments on draft versions of the maps and text were provided by Debbie Sullivan, Joe Eilers, Don Charles, Marty Giles, Sallie Jacobsen, John Phillips, Mel Chase, Kathy Grapel, Don Giles, Bill Hastie, Pete Bond, Monte Turner, Kathy Liska, Mary Ellen Rutter, and Veronica Carnegie. Their suggestions were extremely helpful in our efforts to assemble the most accurate and current information possible.

CREDITS

Map Design:	Joseph Bernert
Map Construction:	Joseph Bernert, Sharon Murfield-Tyler, Dean Tyler
Desktop Publishing:	Jayne Charles
Cover Design:	John Bennett
Printing:	J.Y. Hollingsworth Co.

DISCLAIMER

This book has been designed to provide general information on the locations of natural resources and recreational opportunities along the Oregon coast. Every effort has been made to ensure that this atlas is as complete and as accurate as possible. However, there may be mistakes in content or typographical errors. In addition, the information is current only up to the printing date. It is sold with the understanding that neither the publisher nor the author is responsible for the accuracy of the material contained herein.

Recreating on the Oregon coast provides a great deal of enjoyment, but there also exist many hazards and dangers, some of which are pointed out in the discussions contained in this book. Please heed the precautions, and also use common sense. The publisher and author make no claims regarding the safety of any activities discussed or illustrated in this book. Rather, we attempt to describe the locations where popular recreational activities occur. Please use your own judgment regarding the safety and suitability of any and all coastal recreational activities and locations. When in doubt, consult with local experts regarding the safety of planned activities.

The purpose of the atlas is to educate the reader regarding opportunities for recreation and enjoyment of natural resources. The author, E&S Geographic and Information Services, and E&S Environmental Chemistry, Inc. shall have neither liability nor responsibility to any person or entity with respect to any loss or damage caused, or alleged to be caused, directly or indirectly by the information contained in this book.

HOW TO USE THIS BOOK

The majority of the maps in this atlas constitute a series of 24 sectional maps, each covering about 15 miles of coastline. Together these sectional maps cover the entire Oregon coast, from the Columbia River to the California border. An overview map shows the location of the 24 sections and gives a number for each. These numbers correspond with the numbers at the top of each sectional map, thus allowing easy cross-referencing between the more detailed sectional maps and the smaller-scale overview map of the entire coast.

In most cases, each sectional map is depicted on two facing pages. (The southern coast is an exception, as discussed below). The left-hand page includes a narrow strip map on the left side, which shows the locations of lighthouses, and prime areas for whalewatching, tidepooling, marine bird nesting colonies, and good locations for observing seals and sea lions. The strip map also shows the relative width of the beaches along the section. It is intended to provide a general indication of where the beaches are located relative to rocky headland areas, and which beaches tend to be wide and accessible for walking. Beach widths are not drawn to scale. Please be aware that beach widths change considerably with the daily tidal cycle and following major storms.

In addition to the strip map, the left-hand page also contains either one wide map that covers the area approximately eight to nine miles inland, or alternatively two duplicate narrow maps that each cover three to four miles inland. The wide map provides coverage further inland in areas where the resources commonly considered "coastal" occur at a distance of more than four miles from the ocean. Duplication allows easy presentation of all of the resources of interest, even where they tend to occur in concentrated clusters. The legends for each map are presented in standardized locations between sections. Thus, the map adjacent to the strip map contains information on campgrounds, tourist information centers, stables for renting horses, museums,

aquaria, historical sites, charter fishing outlets, and special interest sites. The next map to the right shows the locations of hiking trails, golf courses, clamming beds, crabbing areas, and exceptional spots for birdwatching and fishing. Where a single wide map is used, all of these resources are depicted on the single map.

The right-hand page is arranged similarly, except without the strip map. The map on the left side of this page shows roads, scenic railroads, lakes and streams. Several of these features are also shown, but less comprehensively, on some of the other maps. The map on the right side of the page shows parks, refuges, research natural areas, marinas, boat ramps, and public access docks.

The presentation is somewhat different for the southern coast, from Bandon southward to the California border. First, each section is depicted on a single page only, rather than on two facing pages, as was done for the more northern sections. This is because most of the southern coast is more remote than the northern and central areas, and the developed recreational resources tend to be less concentrated. A willing explorer will find, however, that the southern coast offers innumerable natural resource-based recreation attractions waiting to be discovered. The second difference is the absence of the strip maps for the southern coast. Because much of the coastal highway is inland from the shoreline on the southern coast, and the terrain tends to be extremely rugged, it was difficult to obtain accurate information on the spatial coverage of southern beaches.

A large portion of this atlas consists of various duplications of the 24 sectional maps. In a few cases, coastal cities require more detail, and a larger-scale presentation, than is achieved on the sectionals. After the series of sectional maps, therefore, city maps are presented for Astoria, Newport, and Coos Bay/North Bend.

The main body of text material is primarily a discussion highlighting the major opportunities along each section of the coast. It is arranged from north to south and is sub-divided into five major segments of coastline. Interspersed throughout the text is a series of special topic discussions. These are presented as inset boxes and provide information on popular activities and resources that do not clearly fit into the geographical framework of the main text. The special topics include tides, tidepools, whalewatching, wildlife, beach safety, boating safety, bicycling, dunes, and fishing.

Following the text, a bibliography is provided which lists many of the interesting and enlightening books available that cover the Oregon coast and various recreational topics. The final section of the atlas includes a series of tables that provide information on campgrounds, golf courses, horseback riding stables, sources of information, boat charter services, marinas, museums, and major annual events. Each of the tables is arranged by location, from north to south, and is intended as reference material. Frequent cross-referencing between text, maps, and tables in this atlas will provide the best and most informative approach to exploring the Oregon coast.

Each of the map symbols used in the atlas is described below. Once the reader becomes familiar with the lay-out of a single section, use of the atlas will be very efficient because the symbols are presented in a similar fashion for each of the 24 sections.

Lighthouse locations are shown. Many are historical sites; some are still in operation; and some are open to the public, although hours are irregular. All are popular photographic subjects. The Yaquina Bay lighthouse is reported to be haunted!

Gray whales pass close to Oregon's shores during their annual migration between Baja California and the arctic. Some of the best places for whale watching are marked on the maps; these are generally located on headlands that jut out into the ocean. The best time to watch the whales is between November and May. See the special topic discussion on page 63.

Tidepools are depressions in the rocky intertidal zone that contain pools of water during low tide periods. They contain a large variety of marine life, which is readily visible to the tidepool explorer. See the special topic discussion on page 60.

Marine mammals, such as harbor seals and Steller sea lions, are common at many places along the Oregon coast. In some locations, elephant seals are also present. Popular areas for watching these animals are depicted along the coastline. Many of these are haul-out areas, where the animals climb out of the water to rest and bask in the sun.

Marine bird nesting areas are found on many of the rocky headland areas and offshore islands. Nesting birds are generally present between April and August, and include gulls, cormorants, murres, and puffins.

Campgrounds and RV sites are mapped. The information for public campgrounds can also be cross-referenced to the tabular information on campgrounds (see page 85).

Tourist information facilities include chambers of commerce and visitor information centers. Other sources of information, such as those operated by the U.S. Forest Service, Bureau of Land Management, National Estuarine Research System, and Oregon Dunes National Recreation Area, are also marked with this symbol and are separately labeled.

Stables for renting horses are often located in close proximity, and provide access, to beach riding. See also the tabular information on page 91.

Museums, aquaria, and principal **historical sites** are indicated, and provide an enjoyable alternative to the outdoor activities covered by the atlas.

Charter boat services provide opportunities for deep sea fishing, river fishing, and whale watching. In some cases, scenic river trips are also offered on sternwheelers or jet boats, and some charter services will take bird watchers out to observe tens of thousands of nesting marine birds on off-shore rocks within the Oregon Islands National Wildlife Refuge.

The **special interest** site is a catch-all category, used to depict the location of resources or recreational opportunities that seemed to us to be noteworthy, but did not fit easily into one of the other map categories. Pay special attention to these. You never know what you might find!

Built-up areas do not necessarily correspond to city limits, but rather to areas dominated by residential or industrial development.

Hiking areas are designated with the hiking symbol. In most cases, the approximate locations and extent of the trails themselves are also illustrated, along with the symbol, using a thin green line. In some places, only the symbol is provided, because there exists a dense network of short trails that do not lend themselves to mapping at this scale.

Designation of **exceptional birding** areas is somewhat subjective. Birdwatching can be good almost anywhere along the coast. We have attempted to indicate some of the best places, based on good diversity of species and/or large concentrations of one or more species or groups of species. Many of these birdwatching areas will be influenced by season and tidal cycle. You are encouraged to check some of the bird books listed in the bibliography for more details.

Exceptional fishing, like exceptional birding, is a subjective designation. Fishing opportunities abound along the coast, including warm and cold water inland fisheries, deep sea fishing, surf and jetty fishing, and some of the best salmon and steelhead fishing in the lower 48 states. We have attempted to designate many of the best areas to try your luck. See the special topic discussion on page 78.

Crabbing areas are found in most of Oregon's coastal bays and estuaries. The symbol is placed in the general portion of each bay where crabbing tends to be best. Crab rings are available for rent in virtually all of the harbor areas, and fish scraps can be purchased for bait. Be sure to check with State fishing regulations regarding size limits and how to tell the males from the females. The latter must be thrown back.

The **clamming** symbol is used to designate the best places to dig clams. On open beaches, the symbol is used alone and indicates locations for digging razor clams. In coastal bays, the symbol is used along with designation of the actual clam beds, using a gold color for the beds. Oregon's bay clams include several species. See the special topic discussion on page 78.

Golf course locations are shown. See the table on page 90.

Roads are presented to some extent on all of the maps, but for each section there is one map showing roads in detail. Unless otherwise indicated, only paved roads are shown. Not all paved roads are included, however. The decision of whether or not to depict a road on the map was based on whether knowledge of a particular road would assist the traveler in locating one or more of the mapped resources.

Rivers, lakes, and **reservoirs** are located, and many are named, on the same map version as the road systems.

—   One **scenic railroad** is in operation, near Tillamook.

☐   **Parks** are illustrated, and are coded by color in terms of jurisdiction.

⚓   **Marinas and moorages** differ greatly in facilities provided. See the table on page 92 for details. Most marinas also have a boat ramp, but a separate symbol is not shown at each marina location to indicate the ramp.

🛥   **Boat launches** provide boat access to many of the coastal lakes and rivers. They are maintained in various cases by the state, county, city, or various federal agencies. Some are privately-owned facilities that can be used for a fee.

⚑   **Public access docks** provide access for fishing, crabbing, or sightseeing on most of the bays, as well as many rivers and lakes.

We have had lots of fun performing field-checks on the accuracy of the mapped items from the Columbia River to California. We have explored nearly every nook and cranny of the coastline, and have investigated and mapped countless resources and recreational opportunities. There is little doubt, however, that some mistakes were made and some items overlooked. Please write and tell us where we can make improvements, either in the atlas layout, or the accuracy of the map depictions. With the help of you, our reader, we will continue to provide the most comprehensive and authoritative recreational atlas for the Oregon coast that we possibly can. We would love to hear from you. Please write c/o E&S Geographic and Information Services, P.O. Box 609, Corvallis, Oregon, 97339. We hope that you enjoy your stay at the coast, and find this book helpful in planning your coastal activities.

OREGON

0   25   50   75   MILES

COASTAL OVERVIEW

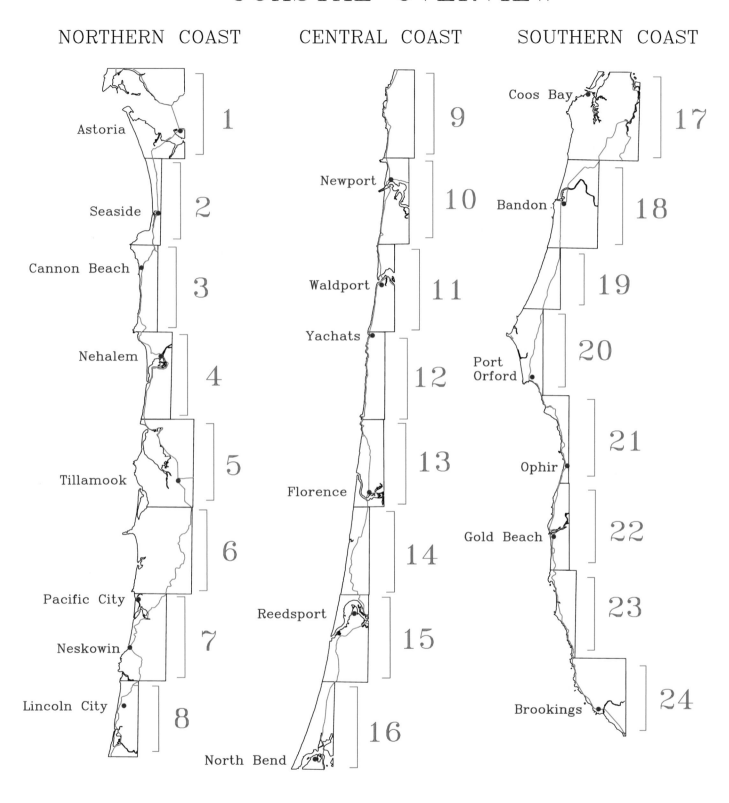

NORTHERN COAST

Astoria — 1
Seaside — 2
Cannon Beach — 3
Nehalem — 4
Tillamook — 5
6
Pacific City
Neskowin — 7
Lincoln City — 8

CENTRAL COAST

9
Newport — 10
Waldport — 11
Yachats — 12
13
Florence — 14
Reedsport — 15
North Bend — 16

SOUTHERN COAST

Coos Bay — 17
Bandon — 18
19
20
Port Orford
Ophir — 21
Gold Beach — 22
23
Brookings — 24

SECTION 1

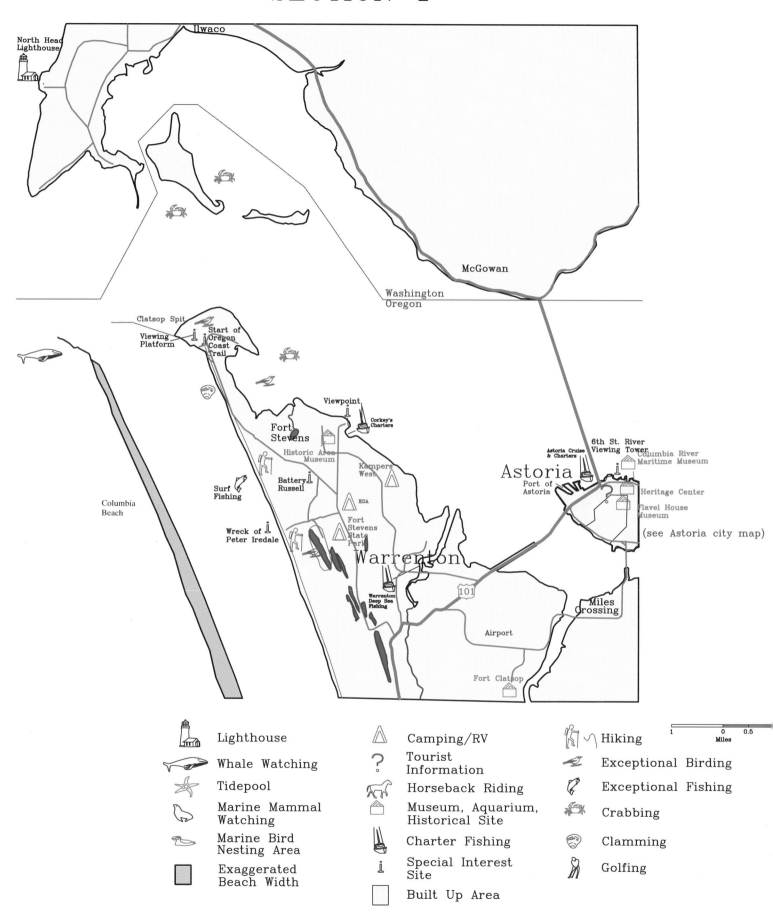

North Head Lighthouse

Ilwaco

McGowan

Washington
Oregon

Clatsop Spit

Viewing Platform

Start of Oregon Coast Trail

Viewpoint

Corkey's Charters

Fort Stevens

Historic Area Museum

Kampers West

Battery Russell

Surf Fishing

KOA

Fort Stevens State Park

Columbia Beach

Wreck of Peter Iredale

Warrenton

Warrenton Deep Sea Fishing

6th St. River Viewing Tower

Astoria Cruise & Charters

Columbia River Maritime Museum

Astoria

Port of Astoria

Heritage Center

Flavel House Museum

(see Astoria city map)

101

Miles Crossing

Airport

Fort Clatsop

Legend

Lighthouse	
Whale Watching	
Tidepool	
Marine Mammal Watching	
Marine Bird Nesting Area	
Exaggerated Beach Width	
Camping/RV	
Tourist Information	
Horseback Riding	
Museum, Aquarium, Historical Site	
Charter Fishing	
Special Interest Site	
Built Up Area	
Hiking	
Exceptional Birding	
Exceptional Fishing	
Crabbing	
Clamming	
Golfing	

1   0   0.5
Miles

SECTION 1

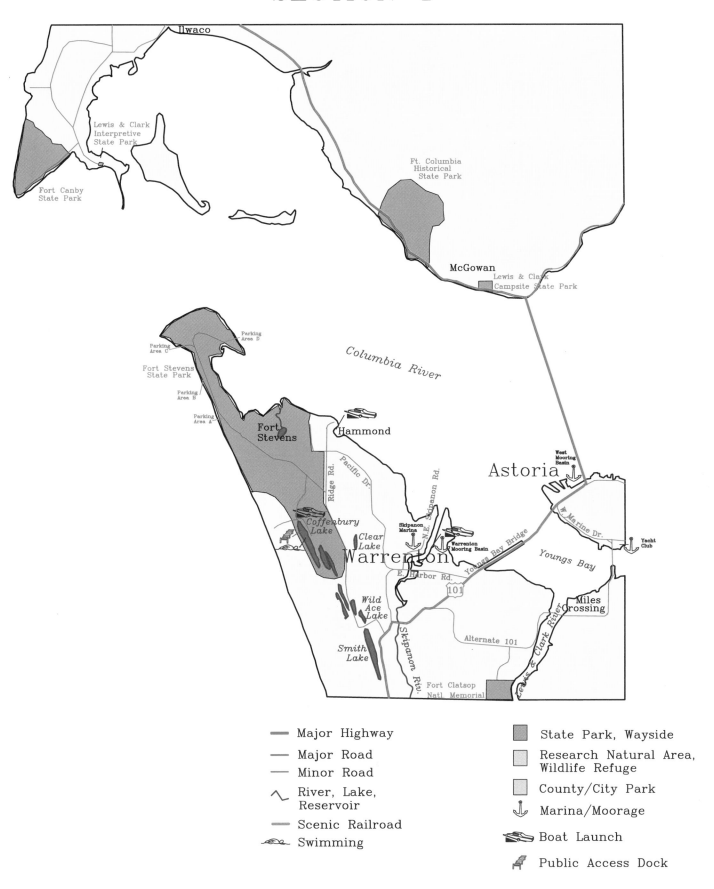

Ilwaco

Lewis & Clark
Interpretive
State Park

Fort Canby
State Park

Ft. Columbia
Historical
State Park

McGowan

Lewis & Clark
Campsite State Park

Columbia River

Parking
Area D

Parking
Area C

Fort Stevens
State Park

Parking
Area B

Parking
Area A

Fort
Stevens

Hammond

Astoria

West
Mooring
Basin

Ridge Rd.

Pacific Dr.

N.E. Skipanon Rd.

W Marine Dr.

*Coffenbury
Lake*

Skipanon
Marina

Warrenton
Mooring Basin

Yacht
Club

*Clear
Lake*

Warrenton

Youngs Bay Bridge

Youngs Bay

E. Harbor Rd.

101

Miles
Crossing

*Wild
Ace
Lake*

Skipanon Riv.

Alternate 101

Lewis & Clark River

*Smith
Lake*

Fort Clatsop
Natl. Memorial

▬▬ Major Highway		▨ State Park, Wayside
── Major Road		▨ Research Natural Area, Wildlife Refuge
── Minor Road		▨ County/City Park
⋀ River, Lake, Reservoir		⚓ Marina/Moorage
▬▬ Scenic Railroad		🚤 Boat Launch
≈≈ Swimming		🪑 Public Access Dock

SECTION 2

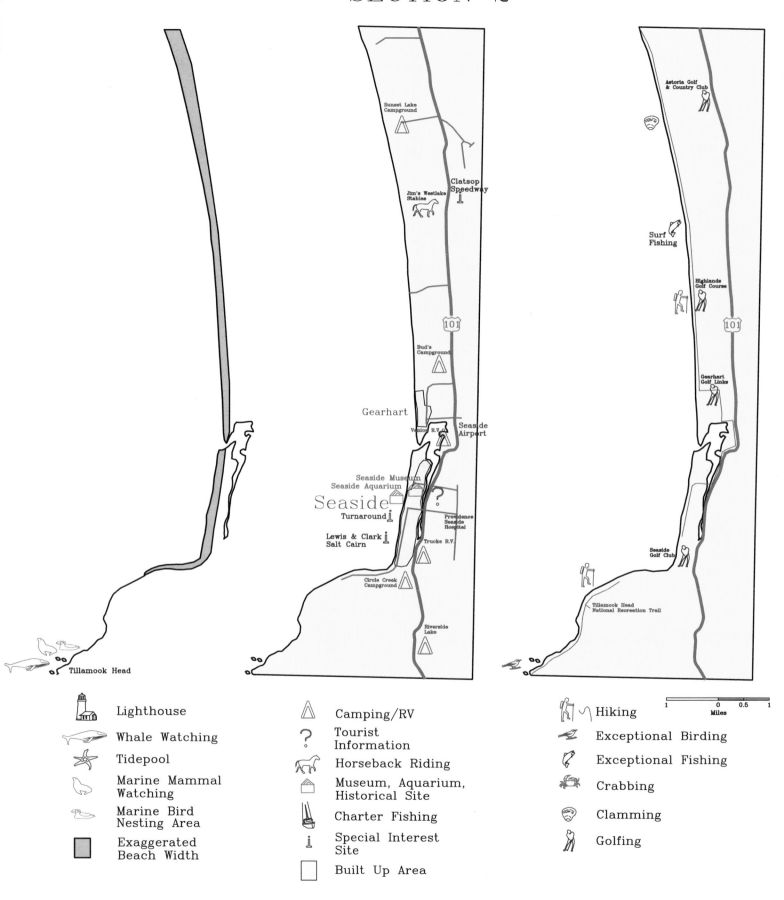

Sunset Lake
Campground

Jim's Westlake
Stables

Clatsop
Speedway

Astoria Golf
& Country Club

Surf
Fishing

Highlands
Golf Course

101

Bud's
Campground

Gearhart

Gearhart
Golf Links

Venice R.V. Park

Seaside
Airport

Seaside Museum
Seaside Aquarium

Seaside
Turnaround

Providence
Seaside
Hospital

Lewis & Clark
Salt Cairn

Trucke R.V.

Seaside
Golf Club

Circle Creek
Campground

Tillamook Head
National Recreation Trail

Riverside
Lake

Tillamook Head

Legend

Symbol	Description	Symbol	Description	Symbol	Description
	Lighthouse		Camping/RV		Hiking
	Whale Watching	?	Tourist Information		Exceptional Birding
	Tidepool		Horseback Riding		Exceptional Fishing
	Marine Mammal Watching		Museum, Aquarium, Historical Site		Crabbing
	Marine Bird Nesting Area		Charter Fishing		Clamming
	Exaggerated Beach Width	i	Special Interest Site		Golfing
			Built Up Area		

1   0   0.5   1
Miles

SECTION 2

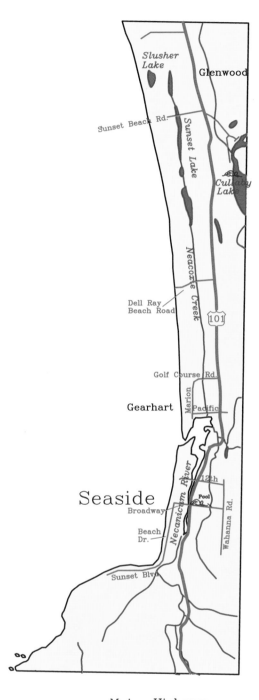

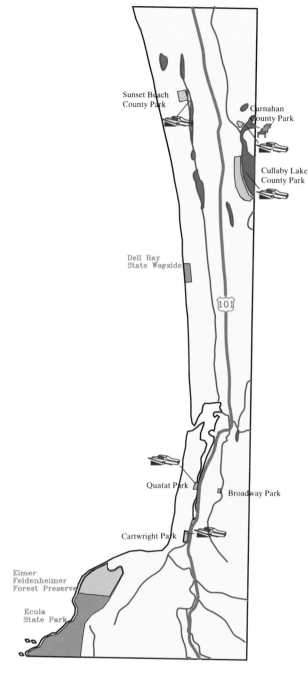

	Major Highway
	Major Road
	Minor Road
	River, Lake, Reservoir
	Scenic Railroad
	Swimming

	State Park, Wayside
	Research Natural Area, Wildlife Refuge
	County/City Park
	Marina/Moorage
	Boat Launch
	Public Access Dock

SECTION 3

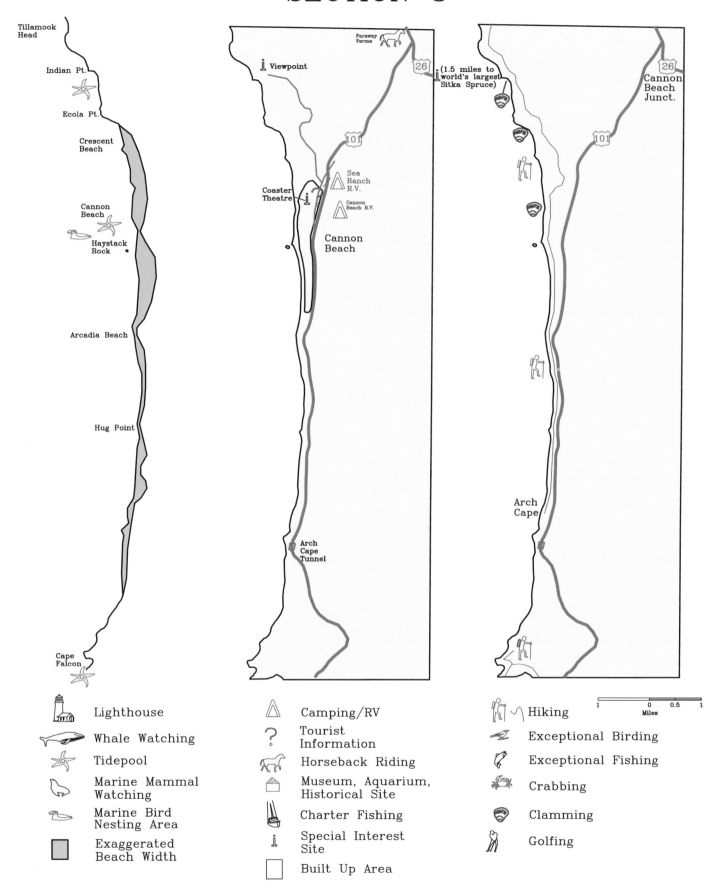

Tillamook Head

Indian Pt.

Ecola Pt.

Crescent Beach

Cannon Beach

Haystack Rock

Arcadia Beach

Hug Point

Cape Falcon

Viewpoint

Faraway Farms

26

(1.5 miles to world's largest Sitka Spruce)

101

Sea Ranch R.V.

Coaster Theatre

Cannon Beach R.V.

Cannon Beach

Arch Cape Tunnel

Cannon Beach Junct.

26

101

Arch Cape

Lighthouse

Whale Watching

Tidepool

Marine Mammal Watching

Marine Bird Nesting Area

Exaggerated Beach Width

Camping/RV

Tourist Information

Horseback Riding

Museum, Aquarium, Historical Site

Charter Fishing

Special Interest Site

Built Up Area

Hiking

Exceptional Birding

Exceptional Fishing

Crabbing

Clamming

Golfing

Miles

SECTION 3

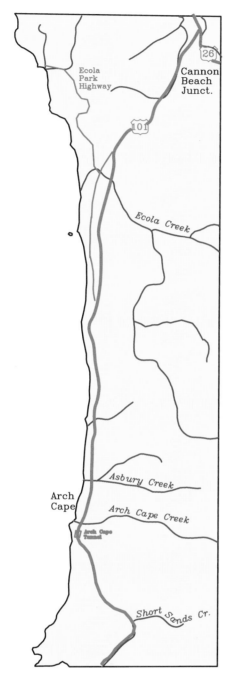

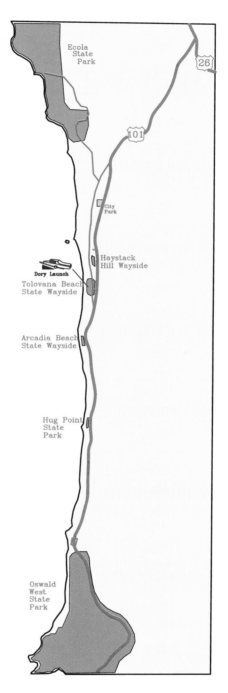

—— Major Highway	State Park, Wayside
—— Major Road	Research Natural Area, Wildlife Refuge
—— Minor Road	County/City Park
∧ River, Lake, Reservoir	⚓ Marina/Moorage
—— Scenic Railroad	Boat Launch
🌊 Swimming	Public Access Dock

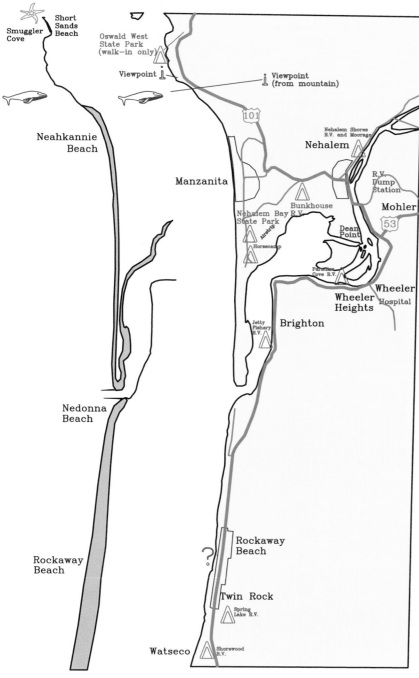

Smuggler Cove

Short Sands Beach

Oswald West State Park (walk-in only)

Viewpoint

Viewpoint (from mountain)

101

Neahkannie Beach

Nehalem Shores R.V. and Moorage

Nehalem

R.V. Dump Station

Manzanita

Bunkhouse

Mohler

53

Nehalem Bay State Park

Airstrip

Dean Point

Horsecamp

Paradise Cove R.V.

Wheeler

Wheeler Heights

Hospital

Jetty Fishery R.V.

Brighton

Nedonna Beach

Rockaway Beach

Rockaway Beach

?

Twin Rock

Spring Lake R.V.

Watseco

Shorewood R.V.

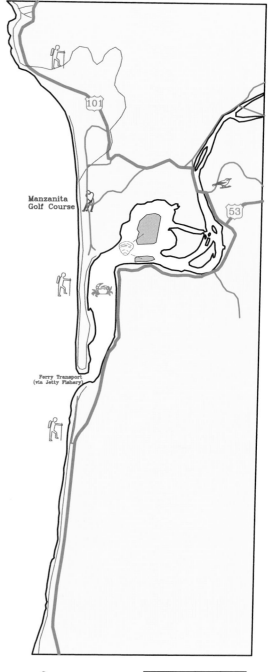

Manzanita Golf Course

101

53

Ferry Transport (via Jetty Fishery)

Legend

 Lighthouse

 Whale Watching

 Tidepool

 Marine Mammal Watching

 Marine Bird Nesting Area

Exaggerated Beach Width

 Camping/RV

 Tourist Information

 Horseback Riding

 Museum, Aquarium, Historical Site

 Charter Fishing

 Special Interest Site

Built Up Area

 Hiking

 Exceptional Birding

 Exceptional Fishing

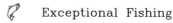 Crabbing

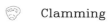 Clamming

 Golfing

1   0   0.5   1
Miles

SECTION 4

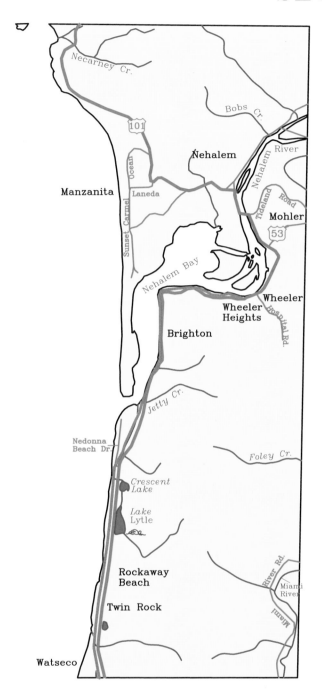

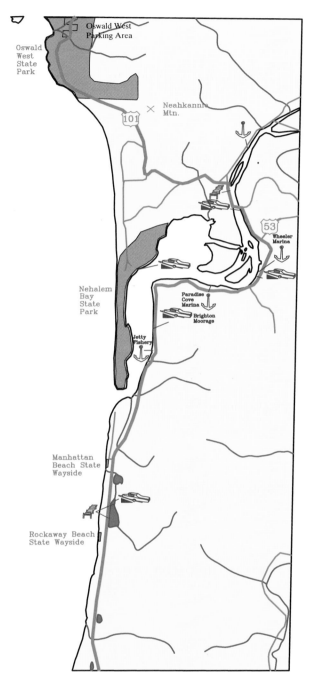

Major Highway

Major Road

Minor Road

River, Lake, Reservoir

Scenic Railroad

Swimming

State Park, Wayside

Research Natural Area, Wildlife Refuge

County/City Park

Marina/Moorage

Boat Launch

Public Access Dock

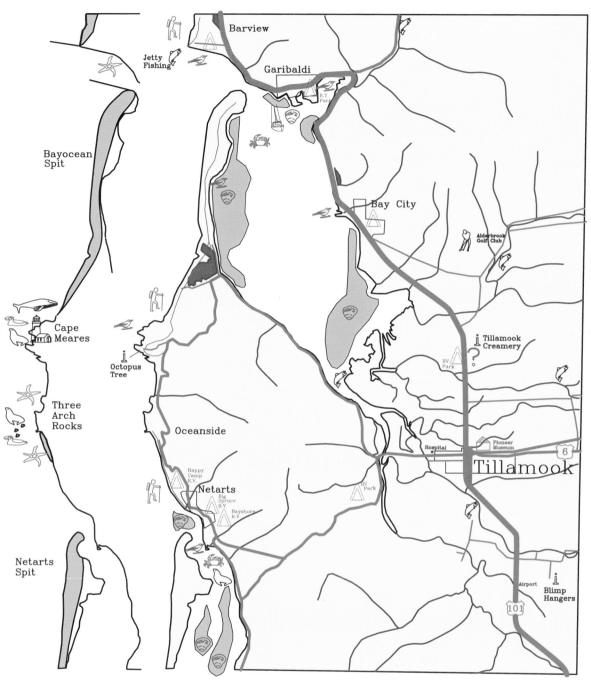

Barview

Jetty Fishing

Garibaldi

R.V. Park

Bayocean Spit

Bay City

Alderbrook Golf Club

Cape Meares

Octopus Tree

Tillamook Creamery

RV Park

Three Arch Rocks

Oceanside

Hospital

Pioneer Museum

6

Tillamook

Happy Camp R.V.

Netarts

Big Spruce R.V.

Bayshore R.V.

RV Park

Netarts Spit

Airport

Blimp Hangers

101

Symbol	Description
	Lighthouse
	Whale Watching
	Tidepool
	Marine Mammal Watching
	Marine Bird Nesting Area
	Exaggerated Beach Width
	Camping/RV
	Tourist Information
	Horseback Riding
	Museum, Aquarium, Historical Site
	Charter Fishing
	Special Interest Site
	Built Up Area
	Hiking
	Exceptional Birding
	Exceptional Fishing
	Crabbing
	Clamming
	Golfing

1   0   0.5   1
Miles

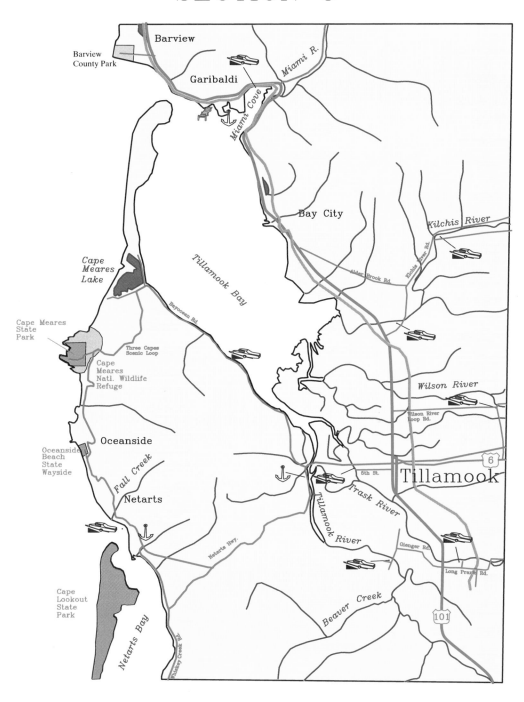

Barview

Barview
County Park

Garibaldi

Miami R.

Miami Cove

Bay City

Kilchis River

Kilchis River Rd.

Alder Brook Rd.

Cape
Meares
Lake

Tillamook Bay

Bayocean Rd.

Cape Meares
State
Park

Three Capes
Scenic Loop

Cape
Meares
Natl. Wildlife
Refuge

Wilson River

Wilson River
Loop Rd.

Oceanside

Oceanside
Beach
State
Wayside

Fall Creek

Netarts

6

5th St.

Tillamook

Trask River

Tillamook River

Glenger Rd.

Netarts Hwy.

Cape
Lookout
State
Park

Long Prairie Rd.

Whiskey Creek Rd.

Netarts Bay

Beaver Creek

101

— Major Highway

— Major Road

— Minor Road

⋀ River, Lake,
Reservoir

— Scenic Railroad

🐟 Swimming

▦ State Park, Wayside

▦ Research Natural Area,
Wildlife Refuge

▦ County/City Park

⚓ Marina/Moorage

🚤 Boat Launch

🪵 Public Access Dock

SECTION 6

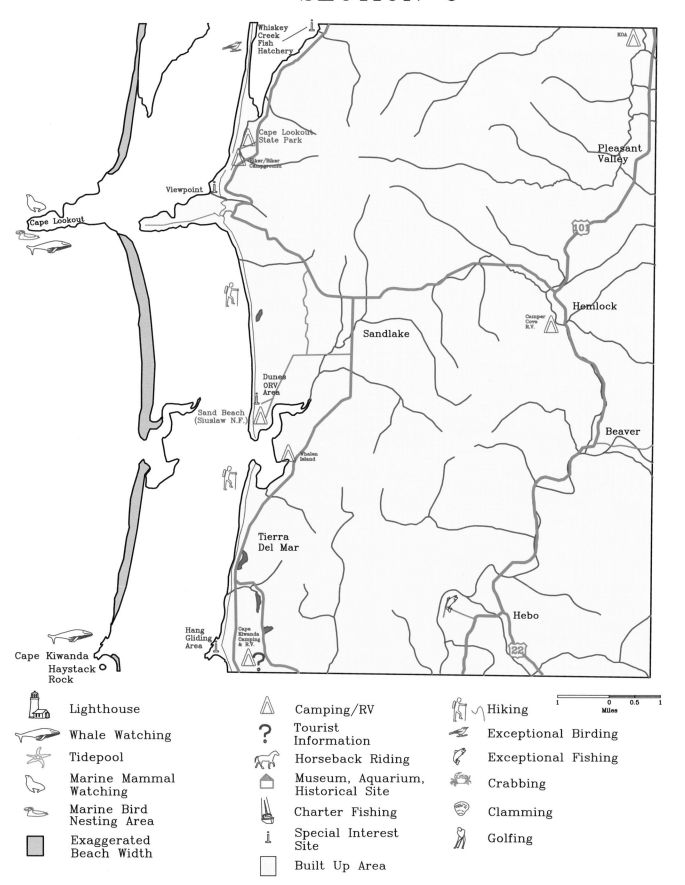

Whiskey
Creek
Fish
Hatchery

Cape Lookout
State Park

Hiker/Biker
Campground

Viewpoint

Cape Lookout

Dunes
ORV
Area

Sand Beach
(Siuslaw N.F.)

Whalen
Island

Tierra
Del Mar

Hang
Gliding
Area

Cape
Kiwanda
Camping
& R.V.

Cape Kiwanda
Haystack
Rock

KOA

Pleasant
Valley

101

Hemlock

Camper
Cove
R.V.

Sandlake

Beaver

Hebo

22

Legend

🏮 Lighthouse

🐋 Whale Watching

⭐ Tidepool

🦭 Marine Mammal Watching

🐦 Marine Bird Nesting Area

▨ Exaggerated Beach Width

⛺ Camping/RV

❓ Tourist Information

🐴 Horseback Riding

🏛 Museum, Aquarium, Historical Site

⛵ Charter Fishing

ⅈ Special Interest Site

▫ Built Up Area

🥾 Hiking

🦅 Exceptional Birding

🐟 Exceptional Fishing

🦀 Crabbing

🐚 Clamming

🏌 Golfing

1   0   0.5   1
Miles

SECTION 6

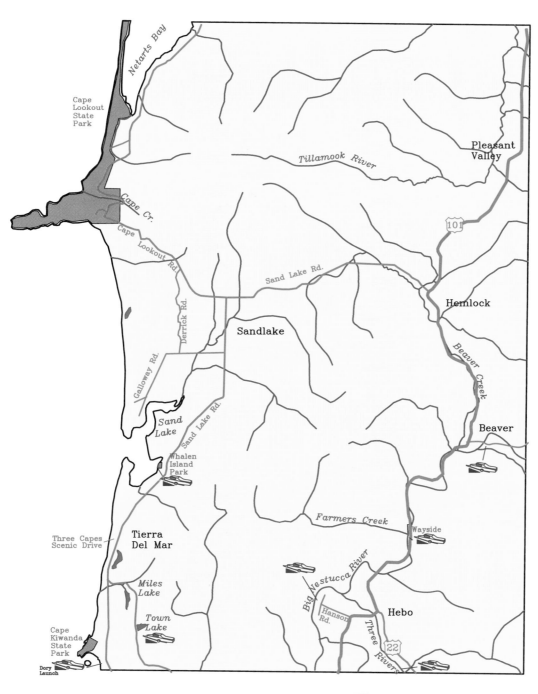

—— Major Highway	▮ State Park, Wayside
—— Major Road	▯ Research Natural Area, Wildlife Refuge
—— Minor Road	▯ County/City Park
︿ River, Lake, Reservoir	⚓ Marina/Moorage
—— Scenic Railroad	🚤 Boat Launch
🏊 Swimming	🪜 Public Access Dock

Map labels:
Netarts Bay, Cape Lookout State Park, Cape Cr., Cape Lookout Rd., Derrick Rd., Galloway Rd., Sand Lake Rd., Sandlake, Sand Lake, Whalen Island Park, Three Capes Scenic Drive, Tierra Del Mar, Miles Lake, Town Lake, Cape Kiwanda State Park, Dory Launch, Tillamook River, Pleasant Valley, 101, Hemlock, Beaver Creek, Beaver, Farmers Creek, Wayside, Big Nestucca River, Hanson Rd., Hebo, Three Rivers, 22

SECTION 7

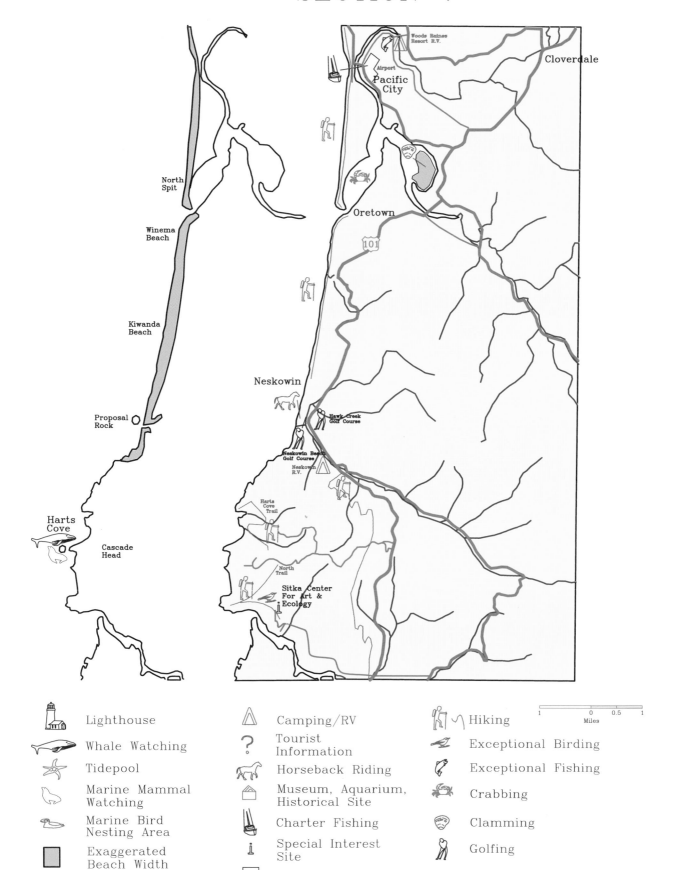

Cloverdale

Woods Raines Resort R.V.

Airport

Pacific City

Oretown

101

North Spit

Winema Beach

Kiwanda Beach

Neskowin

Hawk Creek Golf Course

Proposal Rock

Neskowin Beach Golf Course

Neskowin R.V.

Harts Cove Trail

Harts Cove

Cascade Head

North Trail

Sitka Center For Art & Ecology

Lighthouse

Whale Watching

Tidepool

Marine Mammal Watching

Marine Bird Nesting Area

Exaggerated Beach Width

Camping/RV

Tourist Information

Horseback Riding

Museum, Aquarium, Historical Site

Charter Fishing

Special Interest Site

Built Up Area

Hiking

Exceptional Birding

Exceptional Fishing

Crabbing

Clamming

Golfing

1   0   0.5   1
Miles

SECTION 7

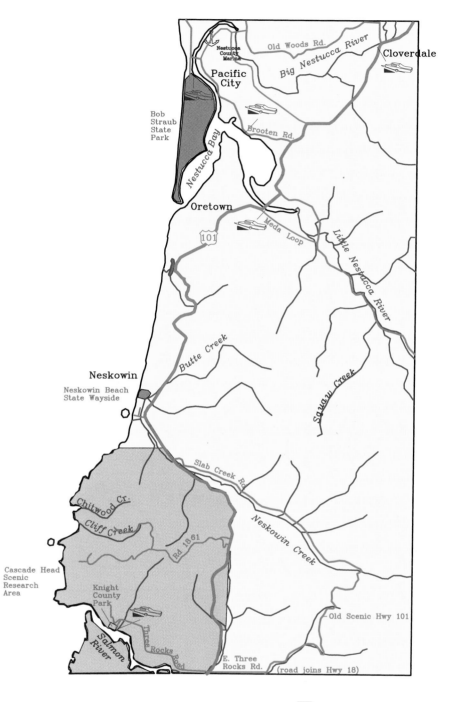

Major Highway

Major Road

Minor Road

River, Lake, Reservoir

Scenic Railroad

Swimming

State Park, Wayside

Research Natural Area, Wildlife Refuge

County/City Park

Marina/Moorage

Boat Launch

Public Access Dock

SECTION 8

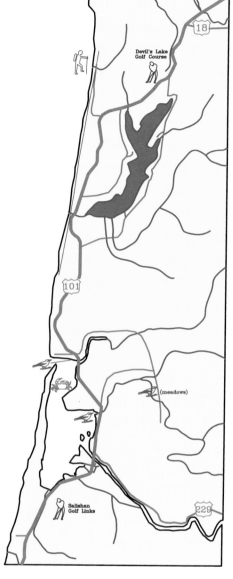

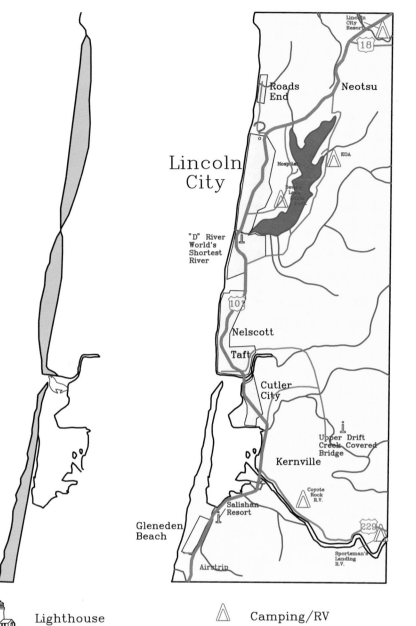

Lincoln
City

Roads
End

Neotsu

"D" River
World's
Shortest
River

Nelscott

Taft

Cutler
City

Upper Drift
Creek Covered
Bridge

Kernville

Coyote
Rock
R.V.

Salishan
Resort

Gleneden
Beach

Airstrip

Sportsman's
Landing
R.V.

Lincoln
City
Resort

Neotsu

KOA

Hospital

Devils
Lake
State
Park

Devil's Lake
Golf Course

(meadows)

Salishan
Golf Links

Legend

 Lighthouse

 Whale Watching

 Tidepool

 Marine Mammal Watching

 Marine Bird Nesting Area

Exaggerated Beach Width

 Camping/RV

 Tourist Information

 Horseback Riding

 Museum, Aquarium, Historical Site

 Charter Fishing

Special Interest Site

Built Up Area

 Hiking

 Exceptional Birding

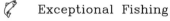 Exceptional Fishing

 Crabbing

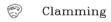 Clamming

 Golfing

1   0   0.5   1
Miles

SECTION 8

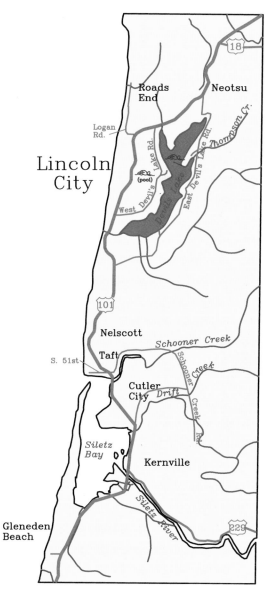

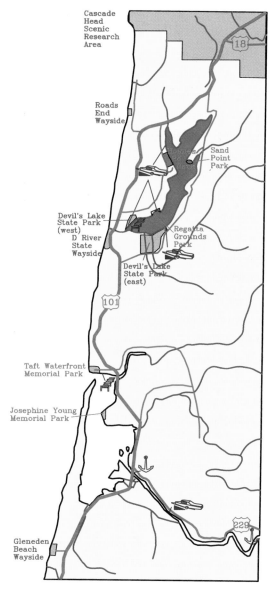

Lincoln City

━━━	Major Highway
━━	Major Road
──	Minor Road
⋀	River, Lake, Reservoir
━━	Scenic Railroad
≈	Swimming

▨	State Park, Wayside
▨	Research Natural Area, Wildlife Refuge
▨	County/City Park
⚓	Marina/Moorage
🚤	Boat Launch
🗻	Public Access Dock

SECTION 9

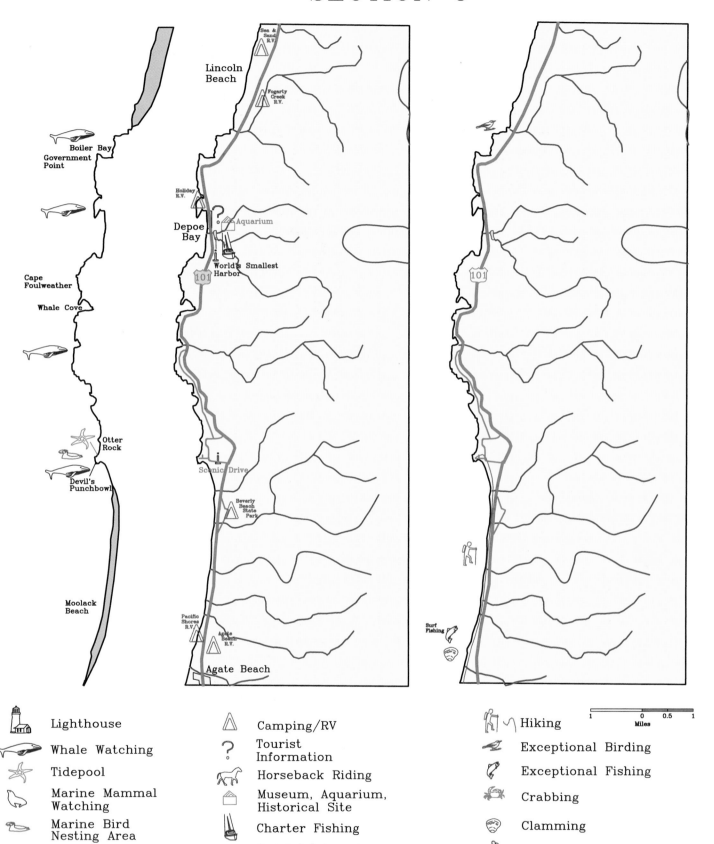

Lincoln Beach

Boiler Bay
Government Point

Sea & Sand R.V.

Fogarty Creek R.V.

Holiday R.V.

Depoe Bay

?
Aquarium

World's Smallest Harbor

101

Cape Foulweather

Whale Cove

Otter Rock

Devil's Punchbowl

Scenic Drive

Beverly Beach State Park

Moolack Beach

Pacific Shores R.V.

Agate Beach R.V.

Agate Beach

101

Surf Fishing

Legend

Lighthouse	Lighthouse
Whale Watching	Whale Watching
Tidepool	Tidepool
Marine Mammal Watching	Marine Mammal Watching
Marine Bird Nesting Area	Marine Bird Nesting Area
Exaggerated Beach Width	Exaggerated Beach Width

Camping/RV

Tourist Information

Horseback Riding

Museum, Aquarium, Historical Site

Charter Fishing

Special Interest Site

Built Up Area

Hiking

Exceptional Birding

Exceptional Fishing

Crabbing

Clamming

Golfing

1   0   0.5   1
Miles

SECTION 9

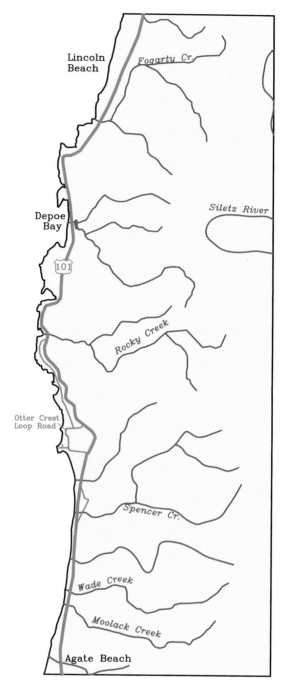

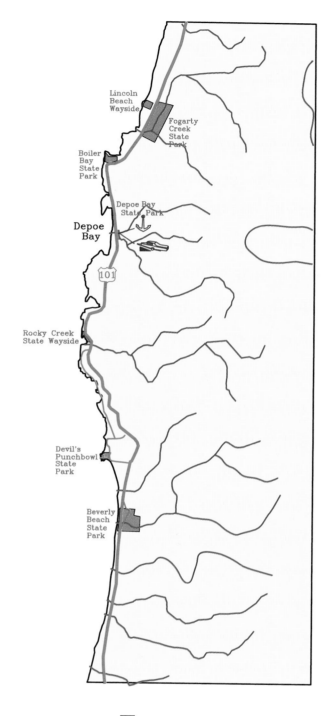

Major Highway

Major Road

Minor Road

River, Lake,
Reservoir

Scenic Railroad

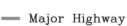 Swimming

State Park, Wayside

Research Natural Area,
Wildlife Refuge

County/City Park

Marina/Moorage

Boat Launch

Public Access Dock

SECTION 10

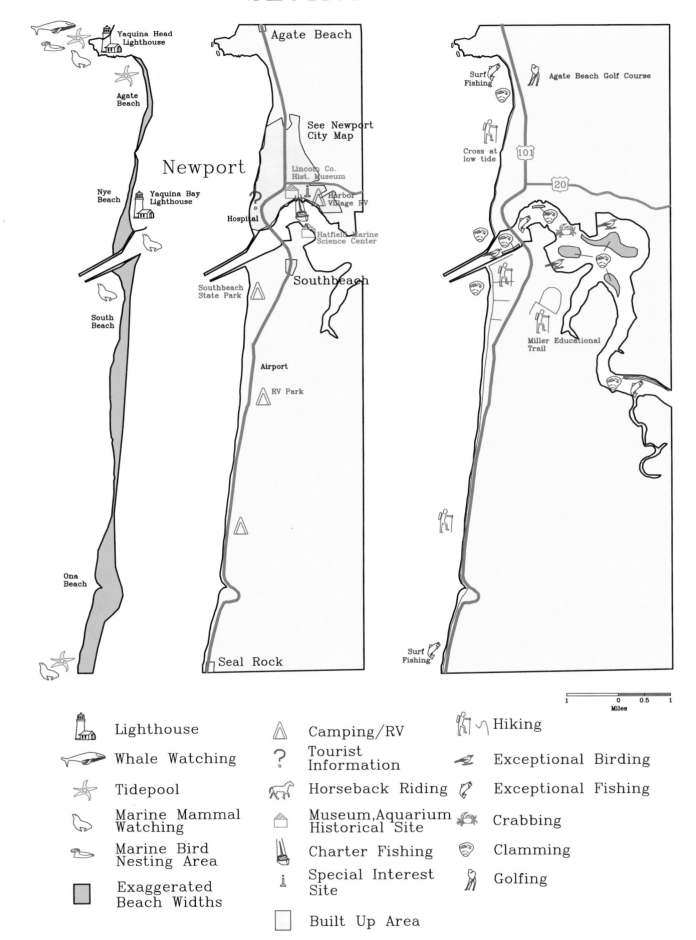

Yaquina Head Lighthouse

Agate Beach

Newport

Nye Beach

Yaquina Bay Lighthouse

South Beach

Ona Beach

Agate Beach

See Newport City Map

Lincoln Co. Hist. Museum

Harbor Village RV

Hospital

Hatfield Marine Science Center

Southbeach

Southbeach State Park

Airport

RV Park

Seal Rock

Surf Fishing

Agate Beach Golf Course

Cross at low tide

101

20

Miller Educational Trail

Surf Fishing

1   0   0.5   1
Miles

Symbol	Legend
Lighthouse	Lighthouse
Whale Watching	Whale Watching
Tidepool	Tidepool
Marine Mammal Watching	Marine Mammal Watching
Marine Bird Nesting Area	Marine Bird Nesting Area
Exaggerated Beach Widths	Exaggerated Beach Widths
Camping/RV	Camping/RV
Tourist Information	Tourist Information
Horseback Riding	Horseback Riding
Museum, Aquarium Historical Site	Museum, Aquarium Historical Site
Charter Fishing	Charter Fishing
Special Interest Site	Special Interest Site
Built Up Area	Built Up Area
Hiking	Hiking
Exceptional Birding	Exceptional Birding
Exceptional Fishing	Exceptional Fishing
Crabbing	Crabbing
Clamming	Clamming
Golfing	Golfing

SECTION 10

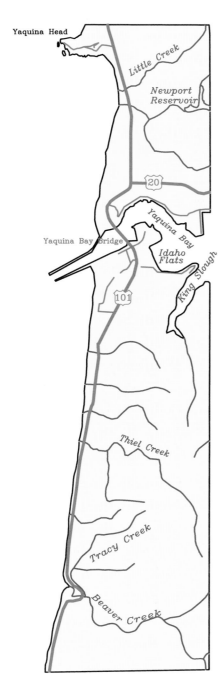

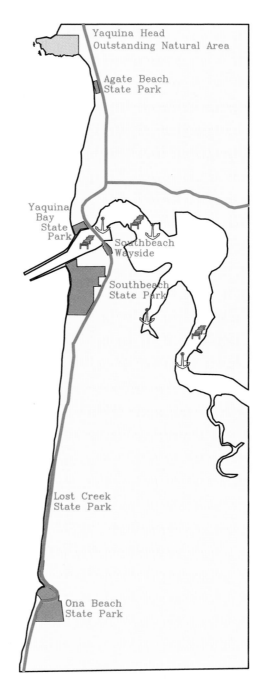

Yaquina Head

Little Creek

Newport Reservoir

20

Yaquina Bay

Yaquina Bay Bridge

Idaho Flats

King Slough

101

Thiel Creek

Tracy Creek

Beaver Creek

Yaquina Head
Outstanding Natural Area

Agate Beach
State Park

Yaquina
Bay State
Park

Southbeach
Wayside

Southbeach
State Park

Lost Creek
State Park

Ona Beach
State Park

— Major Highway

— Major Road

— Minor Road

⋀ River, Lake,
and Reservoir

— Scenic Railroad

🐟 Swimming

▣ State Park and Wayside

▣ Research Natural Area
& Wildlife Refuge

▢ County/City Park

⚓ Marina/Moorage

🚤 Boat Launch

🪑 Public Access Dock

SECTION 11

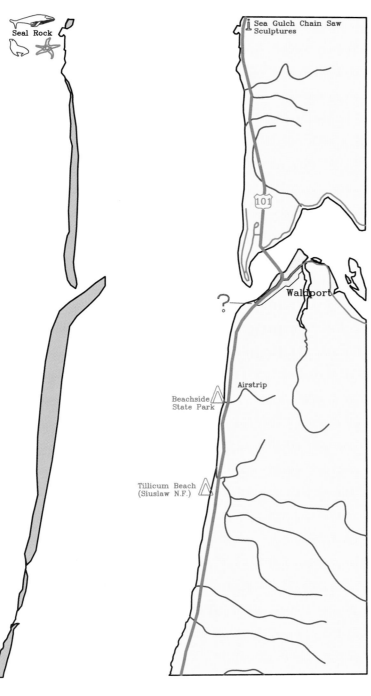

Seal Rock

Sea Gulch Chain Saw
Sculptures

101

Waldport

?

Airstrip

Beachside
State Park

Tillicum Beach
(Siuslaw N.F.)

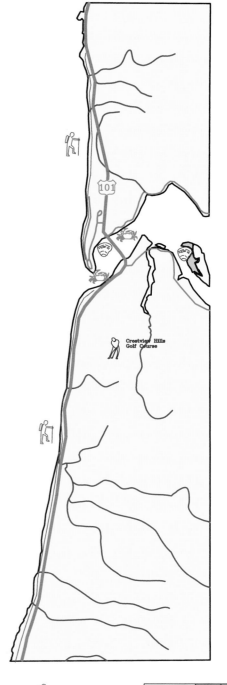

101

Crestview Hills
Golf Course

 Lighthouse

 Whale Watching

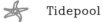 Tidepool

 Marine Mammal
Watching

 Marine Bird
Nesting Area

Exaggerated
Beach Width

 Camping/RV

 Tourist
Information

Horseback Riding

Museum, Aquarium,
Historical Site

 Charter Fishing

 Special Interest
Site

 Built Up Area

  Hiking

 Exceptional Birding

 Exceptional Fishing

 Crabbing

Clamming

Golfing

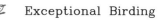
Miles

SECTION 11

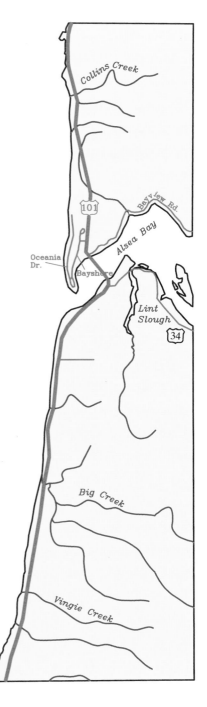

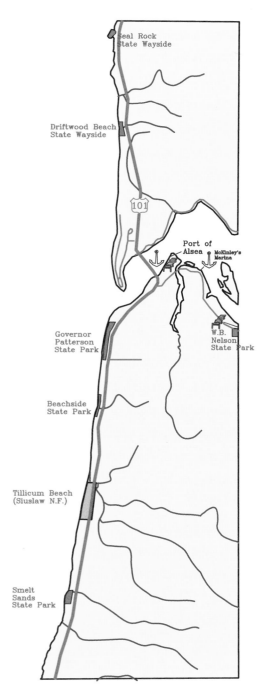

Major Highway

Major Road

Minor Road

River, Lake, Reservoir

Scenic Railroad

Swimming

State Park, Wayside

Research Natural Area, Wildlife Refuge

County/City Park

Marina/Moorage

Boat Launch

Public Access Dock

SECTION 12

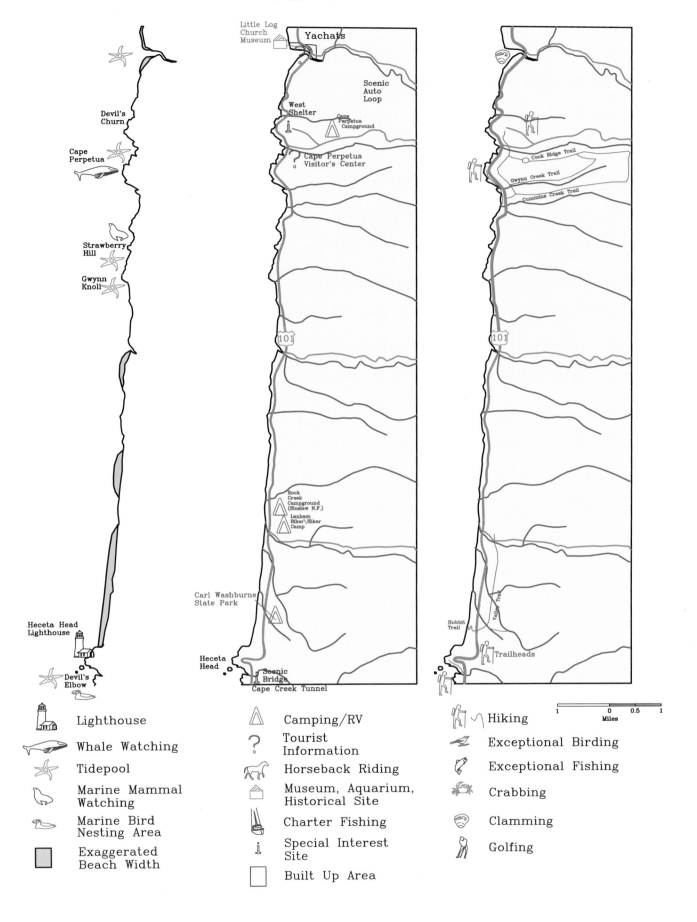

Little Log
Church
Museum

Yachats

Devil's
Churn

Scenic
Auto
Loop

West
Shelter

Cape
Perpetua

Cape
Perpetua
Campground

Cape Perpetua
Visitor's Center

Cook Ridge Trail

Strawberry
Hill

Gwynn Creek Trail

Cummins Creek Trail

Gwynn
Knoll

101

101

Rock
Creek
Campground
(Siuslaw N.F.)

Lanham
Biker\Hiker
Camp

Carl Washburne
State Park

Vista Trail

Heceta Head
Lighthouse

Hobbit
Trail

Devil's
Elbow

Heceta
Head

Scenic
Bridge

Trailheads

Cape Creek Tunnel

Symbol	Description	Symbol	Description	Symbol	Description
	Lighthouse		Camping/RV		Hiking
	Whale Watching		Tourist Information		Exceptional Birding
	Tidepool		Horseback Riding		Exceptional Fishing
	Marine Mammal Watching		Museum, Aquarium, Historical Site		Crabbing
	Marine Bird Nesting Area		Charter Fishing		Clamming
	Exaggerated Beach Width		Special Interest Site		Golfing
			Built Up Area		

1   0   0.5   1
Miles

SECTION 12

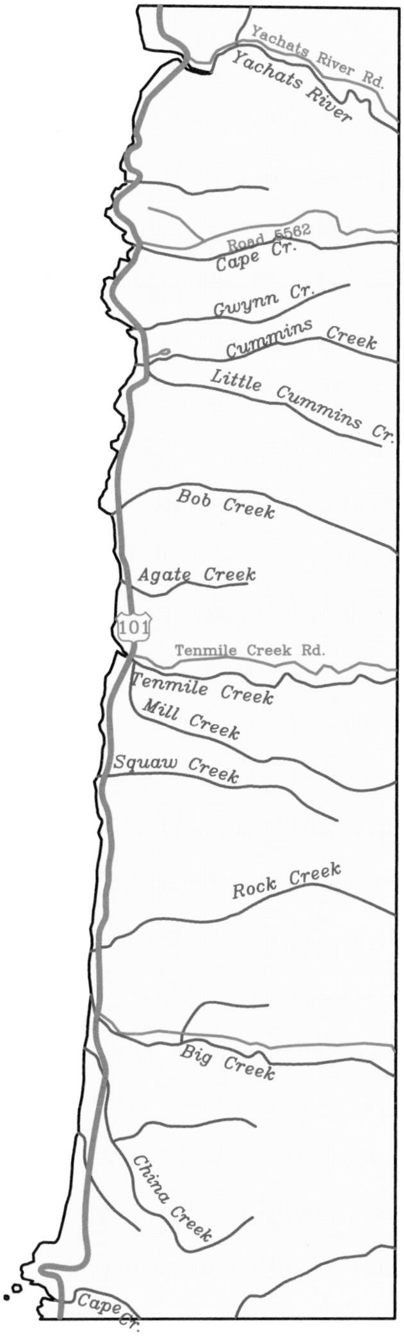

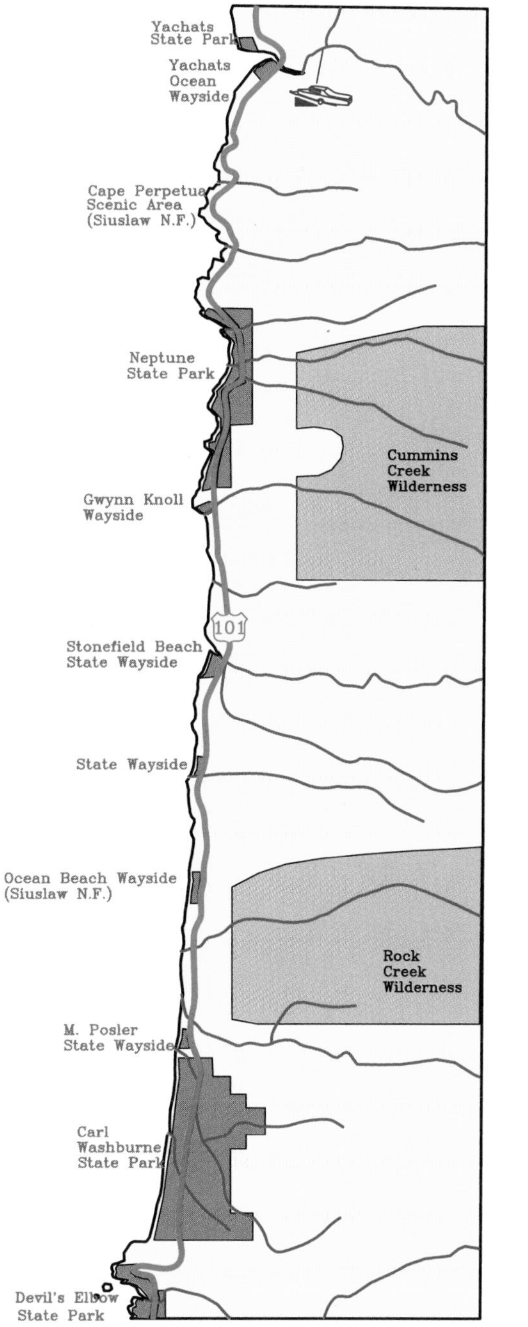

- Major Highway
- Major Road
- Minor Road
- River, Lake, Reservoir
- Scenic Railroad
- Swimming
- State Park, Wayside
- Research Natural Area, Wildlife Refuge
- County/City Park
- Marina/Moorage
- Boat Launch
- Public Access Dock

SECTION 13

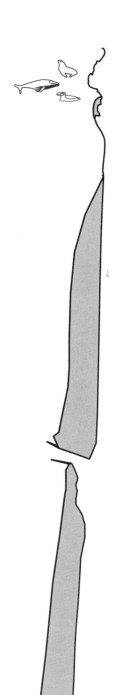

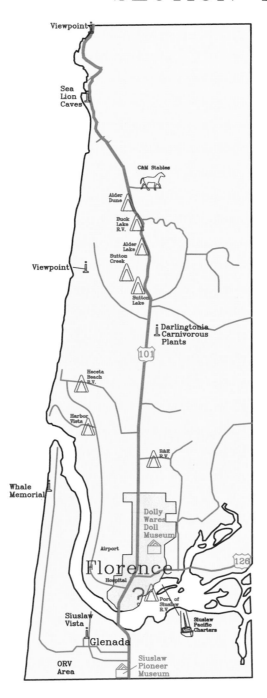

Viewpoint

Sea
Lion
Caves

C&M Stables

Alder
Dune

Buck
Lake
R.V.

Alder
Lake

Sutton
Creek

Viewpoint

Sutton
Lake

Darlingtonia
Carnivorous
Plants

101

Heceta
Beach
R.V.

Harbor
Vista

B&E
R.V.

Whale
Memorial

Dolly
Wares
Doll
Museum

Airport

126

Florence

Hospital

Port of
Siuslaw
R.V.

Siuslaw
Pacific
Charters

Siuslaw
Vista

Glenada

ORV
Area

Siuslaw
Pioneer
Museum

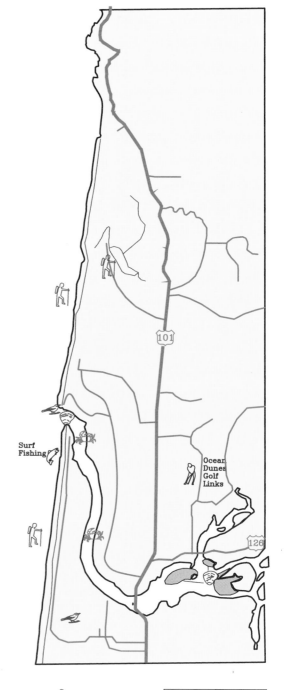

101

Surf
Fishing

Ocean
Dunes
Golf
Links

126

| | Lighthouse | | Camping/RV | | Hiking |

 Lighthouse   Camping/RV   Hiking

 Whale Watching   Tourist Information   Exceptional Birding

 Tidepool   Horseback Riding   Exceptional Fishing

 Marine Mammal Watching   Museum, Aquarium, Historical Site   Crabbing

 Marine Bird Nesting Area   Charter Fishing   Clamming

 Exaggerated Beach Width   Special Interest Site   Golfing

Built Up Area

Miles

SECTION 13

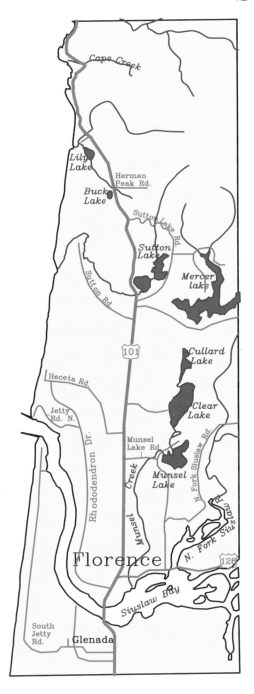

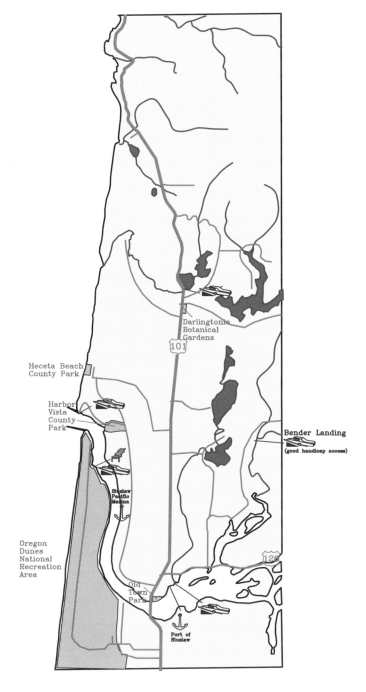

Major Highway

Major Road

Minor Road

River, Lake,
Reservoir

Scenic Railroad

Swimming

State Park, Wayside

Research Natural Area,
Wildlife Refuge

County/City Park

Marina/Moorage

Boat Launch

Public Access Dock

SECTION 14

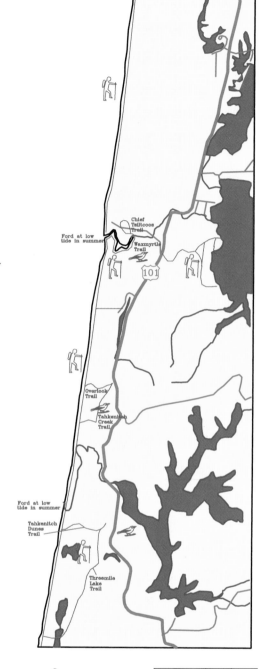

Jesse
Honeyman
State Park

Woahink
Lake
R.V.

ORV
Area

Darling's
Resort

Tyee

Driftwood
II Lagoon
Lodgepole

Waxmyrtle

101

Carter
Lake

Oregon
Dunes
Overlook

Tahkenitch
Landing

Tahkenitch

Boater

Chief
Tsiltcoos
Trail

Ford at low
tide in summer

Waxmyrtle
Trail

101

Overlook
Trail

Tahkenitch
Creek
Trail

Ford at low
tide in summer

Tahkenitch
Dunes
Trail

Threemile
Lake
Trail

(from Overlook)

  Lighthouse

 Whale Watching

 Tidepool

 Marine Mammal
Watching

Marine Bird
Nesting Area

Exaggerated
Beach Width

 Camping/RV

 Tourist
Information

 Horseback Riding

 Museum, Aquarium,
Historical Site

 Charter Fishing

 Special Interest
Site

 Built Up Area

 Hiking

 Exceptional Birding

 Exceptional Fishing

 Crabbing

 Clamming

 Golfing

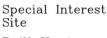
1   0   0.5   1
Miles

SECTION 14

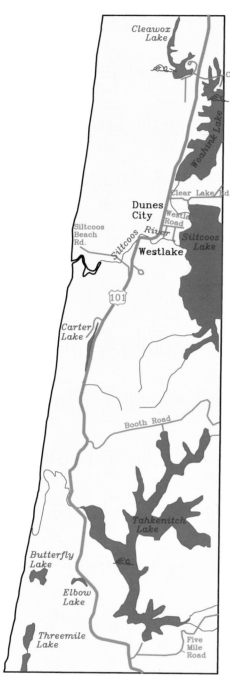

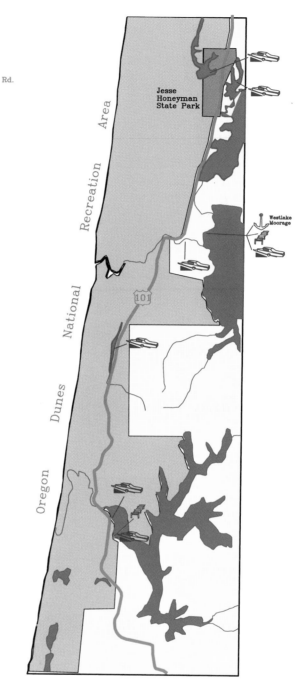

- ━━ Major Highway
- ── Major Road
- ── Minor Road
- ⋀ River, Lake, Reservoir
- ── Scenic Railroad
- 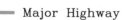 Swimming

- State Park, Wayside
- Research Natural Area, Wildlife Refuge
- County/City Park
- ⚓ Marina/Moorage
- Boat Launch
- Public Access Dock

SECTION 15

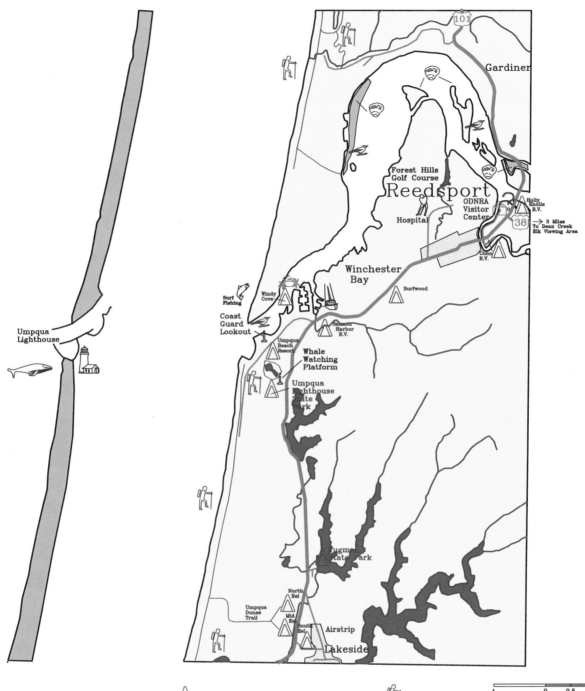

Gardiner

Forest Hills
Golf Course

Reedsport

ODNRA
Visitor
Center

Holly
Knolls
R.V.

Hospital

38

→ 3 Miles
To Dean Creek
Elk Viewing Area

Coho
R.V.

Winchester
Bay

Surfwood

Surf
Fishing

Windy
Cove

Coast
Guard
Lookout

Salmon
Harbor
R.V.

Umpqua
Beach
Resort

Whale
Watching
Platform

Umpqua
Lighthouse
State
Park

Umpqua
Lighthouse

Tugman
State Park

North
Eel

Umpqua
Dunes
Trail

Mid
Eel

South
Eel

Airstrip

Lakeside

Legend

 Lighthouse

 Whale Watching

 Tidepool

 Marine Mammal
Watching

 Marine Bird
Nesting Area

 Exaggerated
Beach Width

 Camping/RV

 Tourist
Information

 Horseback Riding

 Museum, Aquarium,
Historical Site

 Charter Fishing

 Special Interest
Site

 Built Up Area

 Hiking

 Exceptional Birding

 Exceptional Fishing

 Crabbing

 Clamming

Golfing

1   0   0.5   1
Miles

SECTION 15

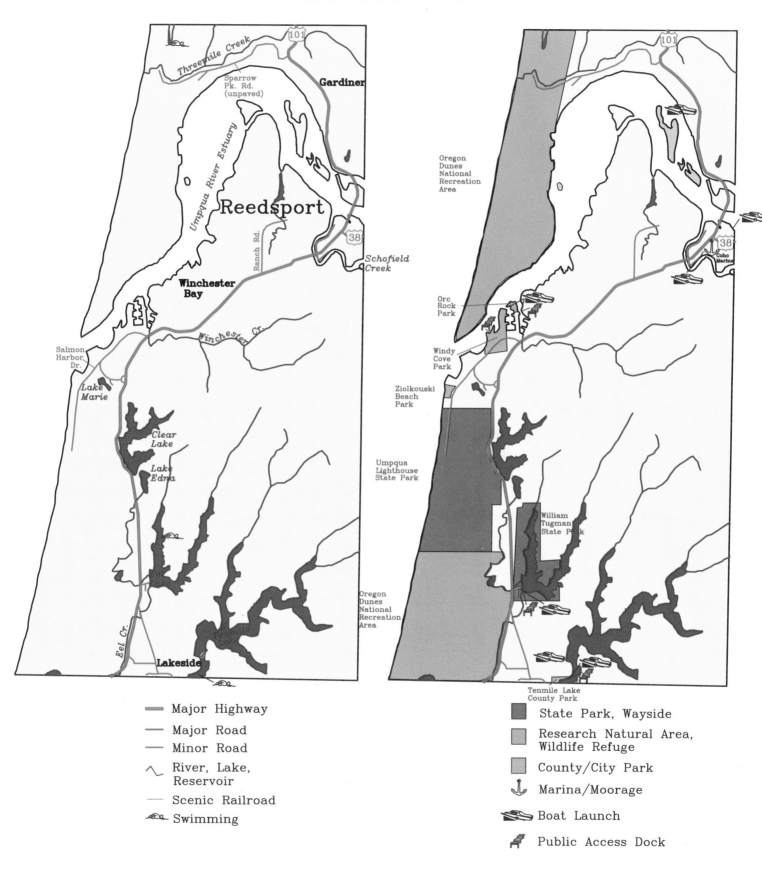

Major Highway

Major Road

Minor Road

River, Lake, Reservoir

Scenic Railroad

Swimming

State Park, Wayside

Research Natural Area, Wildlife Refuge

County/City Park

Marina/Moorage

Boat Launch

Public Access Dock

SECTION 16

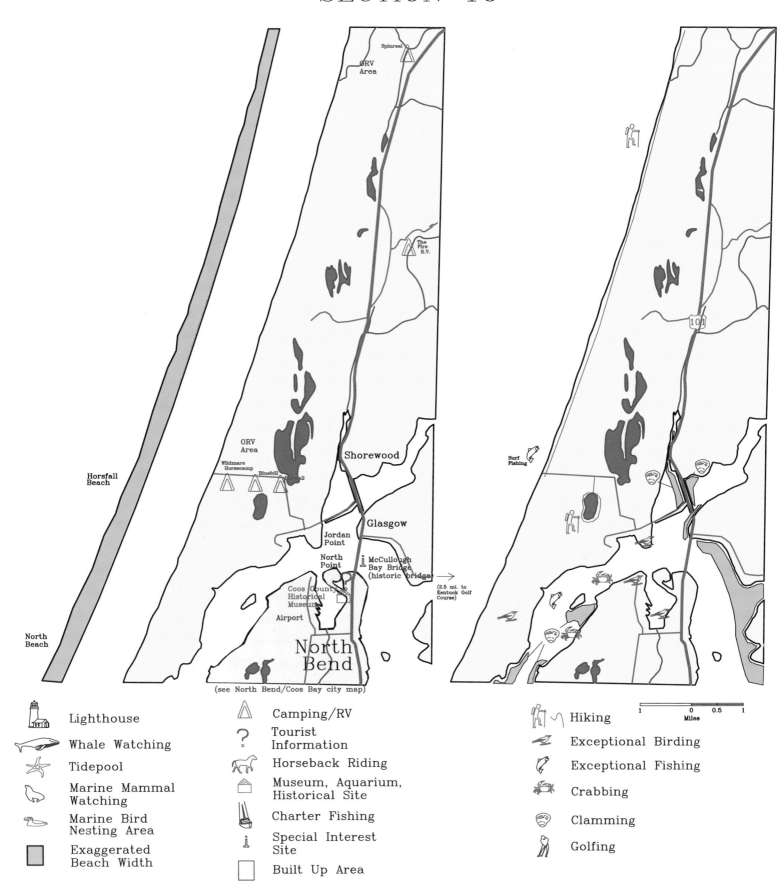

Spinreel

ORV
Area

The Firs
R.V.

Horsfall
Beach

ORV
Area

Shorewood

Wildmare
Horsecamp
Bluebill Bluebill

Glasgow

Jordan
Point

North
Point

McCullough
Bay Bridge
(historic bridge)

Coos County
Historical
Museum

Airport

North
Beach

North
Bend

(see North Bend/Coos Bay city map)

(2.5 mi. to
Kentuck Golf
Course)

Surf
Fishing

Legend

🗼	Lighthouse
🐋	Whale Watching
⭐	Tidepool
🦭	Marine Mammal Watching
🐦	Marine Bird Nesting Area
▣	Exaggerated Beach Width
△	Camping/RV
?	Tourist Information
🐴	Horseback Riding
⌂	Museum, Aquarium, Historical Site
⛵	Charter Fishing
i	Special Interest Site
□	Built Up Area
🥾	Hiking
🐦	Exceptional Birding
🐟	Exceptional Fishing
🦀	Crabbing
🐚	Clamming
🏌	Golfing

1   0   0.5   1
Miles

SECTION 16

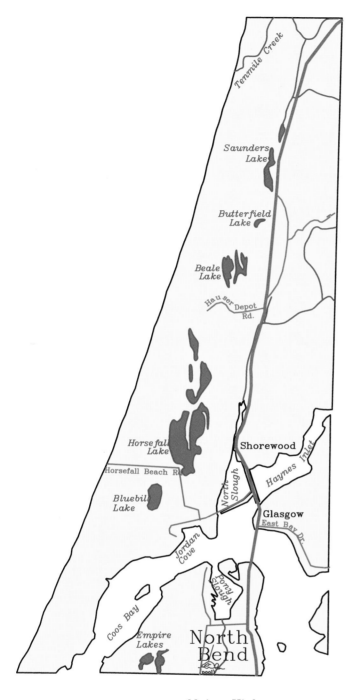

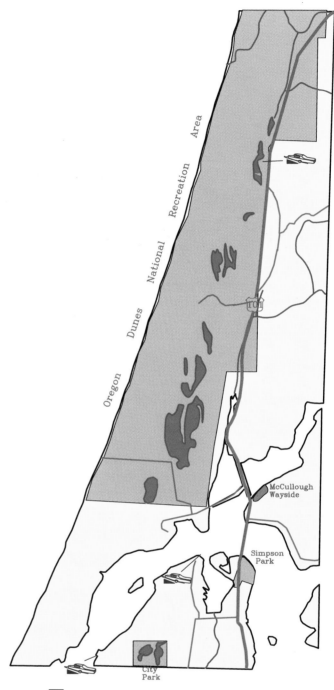

—— Major Highway	
—— Major Road	
— Minor Road	
⋀ River, Lake, Reservoir	
—— Scenic Railroad	
⮢⮢ Swimming	

◼ State Park, Wayside	
◼ Research Natural Area, Wildlife Refuge	
◻ County/City Park	
⚓ Marina/Moorage	
⛵ Boat Launch	
⚓ Public Access Dock	

SECTION 17

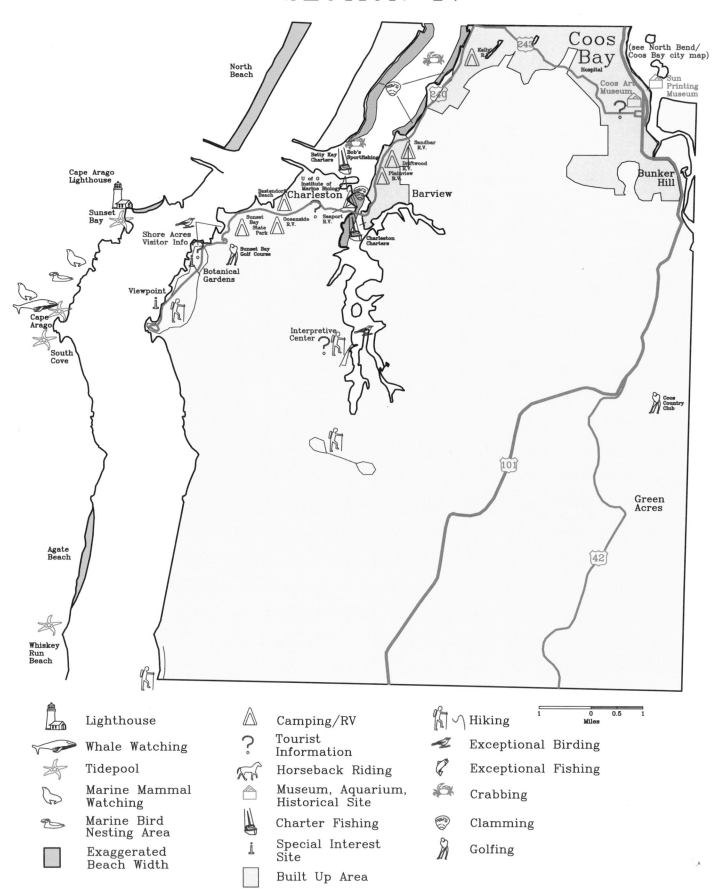

North Beach

Cape Arago Lighthouse

Sunset Bay

Shore Acres Visitor Info

Botanical Gardens

Viewpoint

Cape Arago

South Cove

Agate Beach

Whiskey Run Beach

Coos Bay

(see North Bend/ Coos Bay city map)

Sun Printing Museum

Coos Art Museum

Bunker Hill

Kelly R.

Betty Kay Charters

Bob's Sportfishing

Sandbar R.V.

Driftwood R.V.

Plainview R.V.

Barview

U of O Institute of Marine Biology

Bastendorff Beach

Charleston

Sunset Bay State Park

Oceanside R.V.

Seaport R.V.

Sunset Bay Golf Course

Charleston Charters

Interpretive Center

Coos Country Club

Green Acres

243

240

101

42

Legend

	Lighthouse
	Whale Watching
	Tidepool
	Marine Mammal Watching
	Marine Bird Nesting Area
	Exaggerated Beach Width
	Camping/RV
	Tourist Information
	Horseback Riding
	Museum, Aquarium, Historical Site
	Charter Fishing
	Special Interest Site
	Built Up Area
	Hiking
	Exceptional Birding
	Exceptional Fishing
	Crabbing
	Clamming
	Golfing

1   0   0.5   1
Miles

SECTION 17

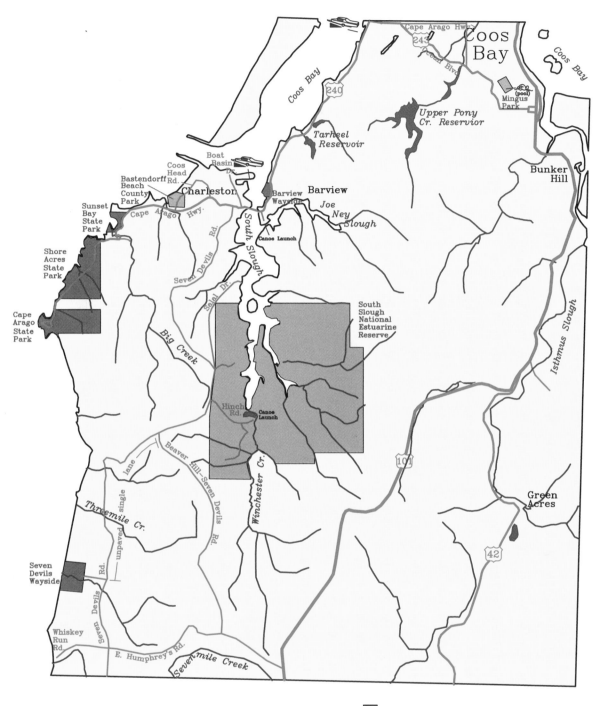

Coos
Bay

Coos Bay

Coos Bay

Cape Arago Hwy.

243

Ocean Blvd.

240

Mingus
Park
(pool)

Bunker
Hill

Upper Pony
Cr. Reservior

Tarheel
Reservoir

Boat
Basin
Dr.

Coos
Head
Rd.

Bastendorff
Beach
County
Park

Charleston

Barview
Wayside

Barview

Joe
Ney
Slough

Sunset
Bay
State
Park

Cape Arago Hwy.

Canoe Launch

Shore
Acres
State
Park

Seven Devils Rd.

Salal Dr.

South Slough

South
Slough
National
Estuarine
Reserve

Isthmus Slough

Cape
Arago
State
Park

Big Creek

Hinch
Rd.

Canoe
Launch

101

Green
Acres

single lane

unpaved single lane

Beaver Hill-Seven Devils Rd.

Winchester Cr.

42

Threemile Cr.

Seven
Devils
Wayside

Seven Devils Rd.

Whiskey
Run
Rd.

E. Humphrey's Rd.

Sevenmile Creek

▬ Major Highway	■ State Park, Wayside
▬ Major Road	■ Research Natural Area, Wildlife Refuge
▬ Minor Road	■ County/City Park
⋀ River, Lake, Reservoir	⚓ Marina/Moorage
▬ Scenic Railroad	🚤 Boat Launch
🏊 Swimming	⌁ Public Access Dock

SECTION 18

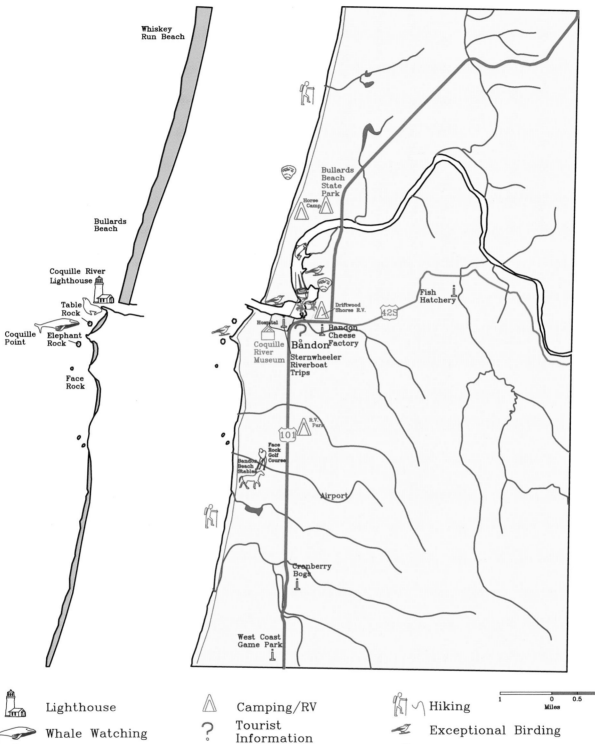

Whiskey
Run Beach

Bullards
Beach

Coquille River
Lighthouse

Table
Rock

Coquille
Point

Elephant
Rock

Face
Rock

Bullards
Beach State
Park

Horse
Camp

Driftwood
Shores R.V.

Fish
Hatchery

425

Hospital

Coquille
River
Museum

Bandon
Cheese
Factory

Bandon

Sternwheeler
Riverboat
Trips

R.V.
Park

101

Face
Rock
Golf
Course

Bandon
Beach
Stables

Airport

Cranberry
Bogs

West Coast
Game Park

 Lighthouse

 Whale Watching

 Tidepool

 Marine Mammal
Watching

 Marine Bird
Nesting Area

 Exaggerated
Beach Width

 Camping/RV

 Tourist
Information

 Horseback Riding

Museum, Aquarium,
Historical Site

Charter Fishing

 Special Interest
Site

Built Up Area

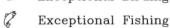 Hiking

 Exceptional Birding

 Exceptional Fishing

 Crabbing

Clamming

Golfing

1   0   0.5   1
Miles

SECTION 18

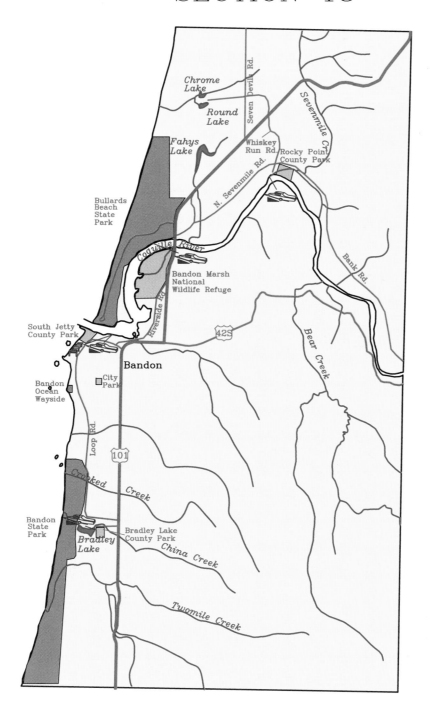

Chrome Lake

Round Lake

Seven Devils Rd.

Sevenmile Cr.

Fahys Lake

Whiskey Run Rd.

Rocky Point County Park

N. Sevenmile Rd.

Bullards Beach State Park

Coquille River

Bank Rd.

Bandon Marsh National Wildlife Refuge

South Jetty County Park

Riverside Rd.

42S

Bear Creek

Bandon

City Park

Bandon Ocean Wayside

Loop Rd.

101

Crooked Creek

Bandon State Park

Bradley Lake County Park

China Creek

Bradley Lake

Twomile Creek

Legend	
—— Major Highway	State Park, Wayside
—— Major Road	Research Natural Area, Wildlife Refuge
—— Minor Road	County/City Park
⋀ River, Lake, Reservoir	Marina/Moorage
—— Scenic Railroad	Boat Launch
Swimming	Public Access Dock

SECTIONS 19 & 20

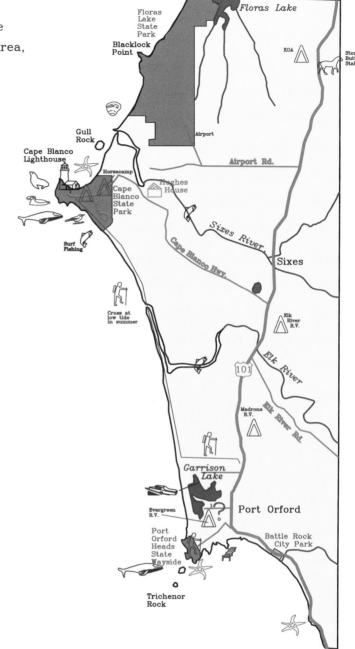

Legend

—— Major Highway	▨ State Park, Wayside
—— Major Road	▨ Research Natural Area, Wildlife Refuge
—— Minor Road	▨ County/City Park
︿ River, Lake, Reservoir	⚓ Marina/Moorage
▬ Scenic Railroad	Boat Launch
∿ Swimming	Public Access Dock

Map labels:
Laurel Lake, Museum of Professional Sports, West Coast Game Park, Lower Fourmile Rd., Fourmile Cr., Croft Lake Rd., Croft Lake, New Lake, New River, 101, Langlois R.V., Langlois, Boice Cope County Park, Floras Lake Rd., Floras Lake Loop, Windsurfing School, Floras Lake

Floras Lake State Park, Blacklock Point, KOA, Stone Butte Stables, Floras Lake, Airport, Airport Rd., Gull Rock, Cape Blanco Lighthouse, Horsecamp, Cape Blanco State Park, Hughes House, Sixes River, Sixes, Cape Blanco Hwy., Surf Fishing, Cross at low tide in summer, Elk River R.V., Elk River, 101, Madrona R.V., Elk River Rd., Garrison Lake, Port Orford, Evergreen R.V., Battle Rock City Park, Port Orford Heads State Wayside, Trichenor Rock

Icon Legend

🗼 Lighthouse	⛺ Camping/RV	Hiking	Exceptional Birding
🐋 Whale Watching	? Tourist Information	Exceptional Fishing
⭐ Tidepool	🐴 Horseback Riding	🦀 Crabbing
🦭 Marine Mammal Watching	Museum, Aquarium, Historical Site	Clamming
Marine Bird Nesting Area	Charter Fishing	⛳ Golfing
	i Special Interest Site	
	☐ Built Up Area	

Miles
1   0   0.5   1

SECTION 21

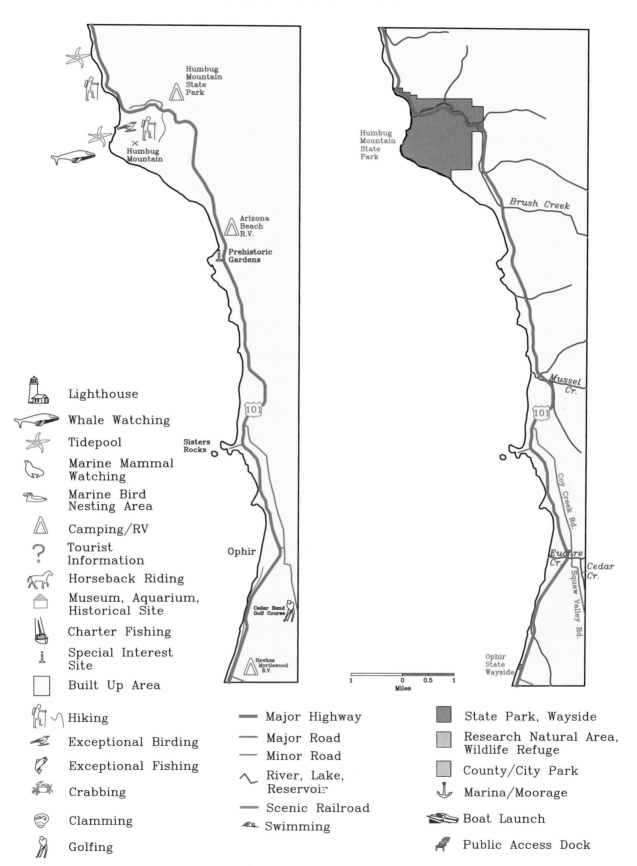

Humbug
Mountain
State
Park

Humbug
Mountain

Arizona
Beach
R.V.

Prehistoric
Gardens

101

Sisters
Rocks

Ophir

Cedar Bend
Golf Course

Hawkes
Myrtlewood
R.V.

Humbug
Mountain
State
Park

Brush Creek

Mussel
Cr.

101

Coy Creek Rd.

Eugene
Cr.

Cedar
Cr.

Squaw Valley Rd.

Ophir
State
Wayside

1   0   0.5   1
Miles

Lighthouse

Whale Watching

Tidepool

Marine Mammal
Watching

Marine Bird
Nesting Area

Camping/RV

Tourist
Information

Horseback Riding

Museum, Aquarium,
Historical Site

Charter Fishing

Special Interest
Site

Built Up Area

Hiking

Exceptional Birding

Exceptional Fishing

Crabbing

Clamming

Golfing

Major Highway

Major Road

Minor Road

River, Lake,
Reservoir

Scenic Railroad

Swimming

State Park, Wayside

Research Natural Area,
Wildlife Refuge

County/City Park

Marina/Moorage

Boat Launch

Public Access Dock

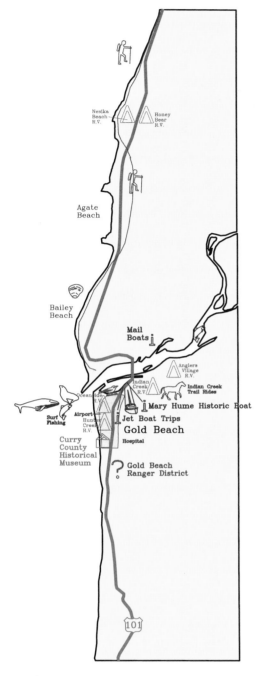

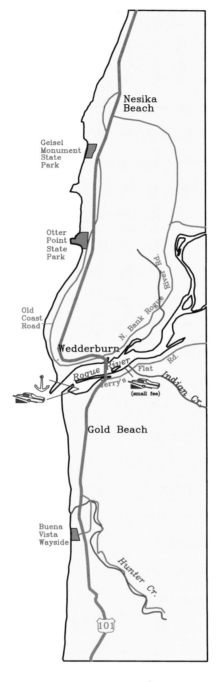

Nesika Beach R.V.
Honey Bear R.V.

Agate Beach

Bailey Beach

Mail Boats

Anglers Village R.V.

Indian Creek R.V.
Indian Creek Trail Rides

Oceanside R.V.

Surf Fishing

Airport
Hunter Creek R.V.

Mary Hume Historic Boat

Jet Boat Trips

Gold Beach

Hospital

Curry County Historical Museum

Gold Beach Ranger District

Nesika Beach

Geisel Monument State Park

Otter Point State Park

Old Coast Road

N. Bank Rogue River Rd.

Wedderburn

Rogue River

Jerry's

Flat Rd.

Indian Cr.

(small fee)

Gold Beach

Buena Vista Wayside

Hunter Cr.

101

101

▬▬▬	Major Highway
▬▬	Major Road
—	Minor Road
∧	River, Lake, Reservoir
—	Scenic Railroad
■	State Park, Wayside
■	Research Natural Area, Wildlife Refuge
■	County/City Park
⚓	Marina/Moorage
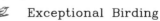	Boat Launch
	Public Access Dock

Lighthouse	Camping/RV	Hiking	
Whale Watching	? Tourist Information	Exceptional Birding	
Tidepool	Horseback Riding	Exceptional Fishing	
Marine Mammal Watching	Museum, Aquarium, Historical Site	Crabbing	
Marine Bird Nesting Area	Charter Fishing	Clamming	
	i Special Interest Site	Golfing	
	▢ Built Up Area		

1   0   0.5   1
Miles

SECTION 23

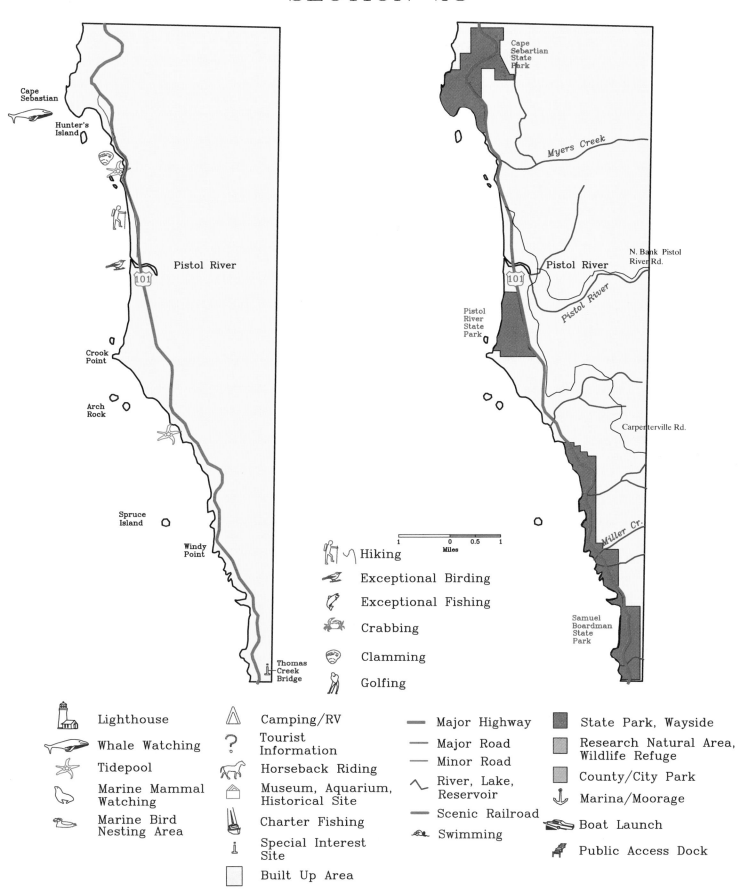

Cape Sebastian

Hunter's Island

Pistol River

101

Crook Point

Arch Rock

Spruce Island

Windy Point

Thomas Creek Bridge

Cape Sebastian State Park

Myers Creek

Pistol River

N. Bank Pistol River Rd.

101

Pistol River State Park

Pistol River

Carpenterville Rd.

Miller Cr.

Samuel Boardman State Park

1   0   0.5   1
Miles

	Hiking
	Exceptional Birding
	Exceptional Fishing
	Crabbing
	Clamming
	Golfing

	Lighthouse		Camping/RV	—	Major Highway		State Park, Wayside
	Whale Watching	?	Tourist Information	—	Major Road		Research Natural Area, Wildlife Refuge
	Tidepool		Horseback Riding	—	Minor Road		County/City Park
	Marine Mammal Watching		Museum, Aquarium, Historical Site		River, Lake, Reservoir		Marina/Moorage
	Marine Bird Nesting Area		Charter Fishing	—	Scenic Railroad		Boat Launch
			Special Interest Site		Swimming		Public Access Dock
			Built Up Area				

SECTION 24

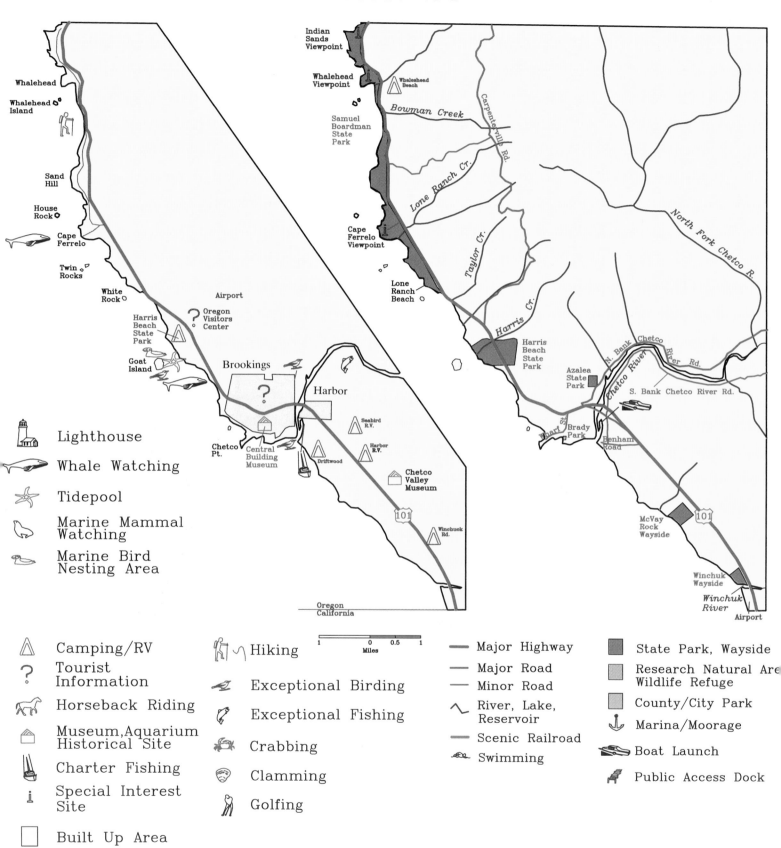

Lighthouse

Whale Watching

Tidepool

Marine Mammal Watching

Marine Bird Nesting Area

Whalehead

Whalehead Island

Sand Hill

House Rock

Cape Ferrelo

Twin Rocks

White Rock

Harris Beach State Park

Goat Island

Airport

Oregon Visitors Center

Brookings

Harbor

Chetco Pt.

Central Building Museum

Seabird R.V.

Harbor R.V.

Driftwood

Chetco Valley Museum

Winchuck Rd.

Oregon
California

Indian Sands Viewpoint

Whalehead Viewpoint

Whalehead Beach

Bowman Creek

Samuel Boardman State Park

Carpenterville Rd.

Lone Ranch Cr.

Cape Ferrelo Viewpoint

Lone Ranch Beach

Taylor Cr.

Harris Cr.

North Fork Chetco R.

Harris Beach State Park

Azalea State Park

N. Bank Chetco River Rd.

Chetco River

S. Bank Chetco River Rd.

Wharf St.

Brady Park

Benham Road

McVay Rock Wayside

Winchuk Wayside

Winchuk River

Airport

Camping/RV

Tourist Information

Horseback Riding

Museum, Aquarium Historical Site

Charter Fishing

Special Interest Site

Built Up Area

Hiking

Exceptional Birding

Exceptional Fishing

Crabbing

Clamming

Golfing

1   0   0.5   1
Miles

Major Highway

Major Road

Minor Road

River, Lake, Reservoir

Scenic Railroad

Swimming

State Park, Wayside

Research Natural Area Wildlife Refuge

County/City Park

Marina/Moorage

Boat Launch

Public Access Dock

ASTORIA

1 Youngs Bay Bridge
2 Tapiola Park
3 Chamber of Commerce
4 Flavel House
5 Fort Astoria
6 Maritime Museum
7 Columbia Memorial Hospital
8 Astoria Column

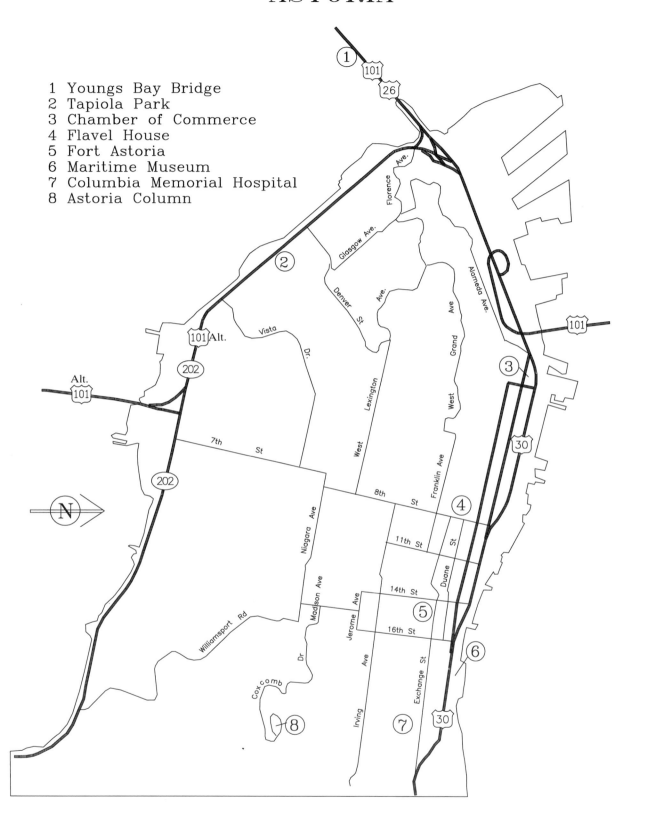

NEWPORT

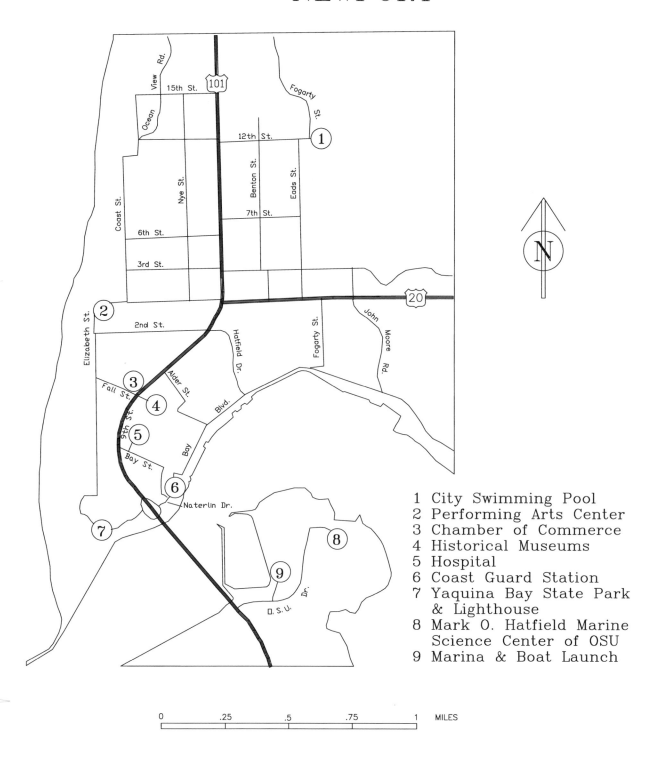

1 City Swimming Pool
2 Performing Arts Center
3 Chamber of Commerce
4 Historical Museums
5 Hospital
6 Coast Guard Station
7 Yaquina Bay State Park
  & Lighthouse
8 Mark O. Hatfield Marine
  Science Center of OSU
9 Marina & Boat Launch

0   .25   .5   .75   1   MILES

COOS BAY / NORTH BEND

1 Windy Hill Court
2 Eastside Park
3 Recreational Vehicle Pumpout
4 Visitor Information Center
5 Visitor Information Center
6 Coos Art Museum
7 Ferry Road Park
8 Windsor Park
9 Coos County Historical Society
10 Simpson Park & Arboretum
11 Lincoln Square (park)

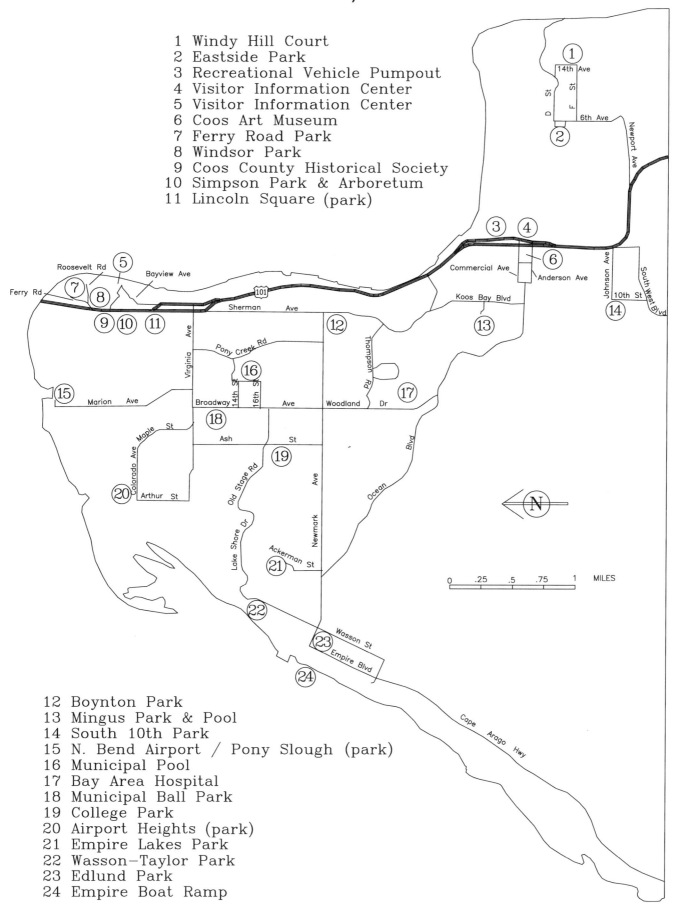

12 Boynton Park
13 Mingus Park & Pool
14 South 10th Park
15 N. Bend Airport / Pony Slough (park)
16 Municipal Pool
17 Bay Area Hospital
18 Municipal Ball Park
19 College Park
20 Airport Heights (park)
21 Empire Lakes Park
22 Wasson–Taylor Park
23 Edlund Park
24 Empire Boat Ramp

TOUR OF THE COAST

INTRODUCTION

The Oregon coastline is exposed to the largest stretch of open ocean on earth. Waves have about 6,000 miles of clear sailing in which to build up strength before colliding with Oregon's 360-mile coastline. The coast alternates between rugged, rocky headlands and long, smooth beaches. The Pacific Ocean is at its best here during major winter storms when Oregon's coast is pummeled with nature's unleashed fury. Pleasant sunny days in spring, summer, and fall enhance some of the finest coastal scenery in the United States.

Abundant rainfall in the Coast Range mountains to the east provides ideal conditions for lush coniferous forests and a multitude of fast flowing, pristine coastal rivers and streams. Many of the latter contain bountiful populations of salmon, steelhead, and sea-run cutthroat trout. The forests in this region are among the most productive anywhere in the world, and some old-growth stands are well over 400 years old. The resulting combination of untamed Pacific Ocean, spectacular rivers, lakes, forests, beaches, and sand dunes, coupled with deep sea and freshwater fishing, clamming, crabbing, swimming, boating, hiking, golfing, wildlife watching, and camping opportunities provide the backdrop for one of the finest vacation spots on earth.

The coastal climate is mild, with wet winters and reasonably dry, sunny summers. Temperature extremes are rare, although visitors should be prepared for cool winds at any time of year. Oregonians flock to the coast in summer to enjoy the coastal resources and escape the heat of the inland valleys. Out-of-state visitors have traveled the coastal corridor in large numbers for decades.

In the following pages, you will experience a tour of the Oregon coast, beginning on the banks of the Columbia River and continuing southward to the California border. Along the way, you will learn of a multitude of natural resources and recreational opportunities. The discussion focusses on what there is to do at the coast and where to do it. Hotels, restaurants, and shops are not discussed, but are covered in other coastal publications. We believe that visitors travel to the coast for the natural resources and associated recreational experiences. Consequently, these are the issues that we focus upon.

Please recognize that the Oregon coast is one of the finest recreational playgrounds in the United States. Vast sections have been set aside as parks, wildlife refuges, preserves, and research natural areas. Despite a booming tourist industry, much of the coast is still extremely pristine and unspoiled. Take a few moments to consider the intrinsic value of the coastal resources, the fragility of coastal ecosystems, and the need to preserve these resources and opportunities for future generations. If all of our visitors will treat the Oregon coast with concern and respect, our children's children will enjoy the same wonderful experiences that we do today.

COLUMBIA RIVER TO ROCKAWAY BEACH

Our tour begins at Oregon's northern border, along the route taken by the mighty Columbia River. The current of this four- to five-mile wide river collides with the sea to form 25-foot breakers in the shallow waters of the Columbia River bar. This is one of the most dangerous bars in the world, as evidenced by the hundreds of vessels that have met their demise here over the last century and a half. Clatsop Spit, a narrow peninsula of sand, juts out on the south bank, terminating in a long rock jetty. The jetty was built to provide some protection for ships in the mouth of the river and to enhance the scouring action of the river, thereby reducing the need for dredging of the main channel. The beach along Clatsop Spit is one of the best in the state for digging

TIDES

Tides are large periodic waves caused by the gravitational pull of the sun and moon. These waves raise and lower the height of the water line by an amount that depends on the location of the sun and the moon in relation to the earth. Tide levels, therefore, change each day. There are two high tides and two low tides daily on the Oregon coast. Coastal recreationists are well-advised to carry a copy of the current tide table, available at sporting goods stores and fishing concerns throughout the coastal area, because tides can have a large influence on many coastal recreational activities. First and foremost, consult the tide table before venturing too far out on rocks or pilings or along beaches sandwiched between cliffs and sea. These areas can be totally submerged when the tide comes in. A leisurely stroll for a couple of miles along hard-paved wet sand at low tide can set the stage for a much longer, and far more difficult, return trip through deep, dry sand at high tide. The hiking time can differ by a factor of about three. Tides also influence birding. Shorebirds often concentrate in large numbers in the relatively small areas of exposed mudflat remaining at high tide; when the tide is out, the birds disperse across a much larger area. You won't see much in a tide pool at high tide. But if you schedule your tidepooling to coincide with an unusually low tide, you will see an amazing diversity of marine life and numerous creatures that spend almost all of their life well under water. Fishermen know the importance of tides to the feeding behavior of coastal fish, and time their outings accordingly.

Although the Pacific Ocean is far too cold in Oregon for all but the most hardy swimmers, those who venture into the surf should avoid outgoing tides. Unfortunately, many people over the years have not realized this, and have been pulled out to sea by the strong currents. Also, use caution near the water's edge; the combination of unusually large (sneaker) waves and rip currents sometimes pulls people off the shore itself!

Tides are measured in relation to the average of all the daily *low* tides that occur during the year. This average is designated as the zero level tide. All tides are expressed as their vertical height (in feet) above or below the zero tide. A -2.0, therefore, is two feet below the average daily lowest low tide, whereas a +2.0 is two feet above the average low tide. Sea level off Oregon is about +4.1, and is adjusted every 19 years.

When the sun and moon are in a straight line with the earth, their gravitational pulls add together, and the tidal fluctuations are large. These are called spring tides (not referring to the spring season) and occur when the moon is new or full. When the sun and moon are at right angles to each other, as viewed from the earth, the tides are smaller. These are called neap tides and occur with quarter moons.

Pick up a copy of a tide table while you are at the coast, and familiarize yourself with how to read it. Any fisherman will be glad to help. A little time spent checking on the tides, and scheduling your coastal activities accordingly, will be time well-spent and will maximize your enjoyment of the coastal resources.

razor clams. Spring minus tides are best, especially tides lower than -1.0.

Fort Stevens State Park contains the largest campground in the state, with over 600 campsites, miles of open beach, bike trails, hiking trails, a freshwater lake for swimming, great beachcombing and birdwatching, and to top it all off, its own shipwreck. The park is divided into three areas: the historical area in the north, day-use area in the center, and campground at the southern entrance. The bow section of the *Peter Iredale* has been on the beach of Clatsop Spit since the 278-foot, four-masted British vessel went aground in 1906 while enroute from Mexico to Portland. Her crew of 27 was rescued. At low tide you can walk around the remains, in contrast to virtually all other Oregon shipwrecks which have long-since been reclaimed by the sea. The viewing platform in the park is one of the best birdwatching areas on the coast, particularly for pelagic (those that live in the open ocean) species and during spring and fall migrations. The small ponds north and west of the parking area are excellent for shorebirds at high tide. At low tide, the bay to the east provides exceptional birding.

Swimming, boating and trout fishing are all popular activities at Coffenbury Lake. There are also more than six miles of hiking trails and nine miles of paved bicycle trails to enjoy in the park. The two-mile trail around the lake originates in the parking lot at the north end. Birding opportunities abound, especially in spring. The west side contains a coniferous forest and the east side a marshy area with dense shrubs. Warbler concentrations are very high during spring migration.

The south jetty of the Columbia River marks the beginning of the Oregon Coast Trail, a hiking trail that will eventually extend the entire length of the state. The northern 62 miles of trail have been completed, as well as several other shorter sections. From the south jetty to Gearhart is an enjoyable 15 mile hike along wide beaches, best done with overnight camping at Sunset Lake.

A few miles inland, on the banks of the Columbia River, lies Astoria, the oldest city on the Oregon coast. Although recreational opportunities abound, don't overlook the region's rich history, with its museums and historical sites. John Jacob Astor's Pacific Fur Company was organized nearly two centuries ago to facilitate fur trading along the Columbia River. The company constructed Fort Astoria in 1811, which became the first permanent American settlement in the West. Since then, Astoria has centered at various times on the fur trade, logging, and fishing. All have declined substantially since their respective heydays.

Astoria contains dozens of beautiful Victorian homes built in the latter half of the nineteenth century, especially along Franklin Avenue between 7th and 17th streets and around Grand Avenue and 16th Street. Many are listed in the National Register of Historic Places. Flavel House, a Queen Anne style mansion, is open to the public as a museum and showcases the exquisite architecture and furniture of the period. Stop by the visitor information center and pick up a walking tour guide of the historic district.

The Columbia River Maritime Museum and lightship *Columbia* moored next door at the Coast Guard dock are well worth the visit for all would-be "old salts". The Maritime Museum is one of the best, and includes exhibits of shipwreck remains, model ships, fishing equipment, whaling artifacts, and other reminders of the nautical history of this region.

A trip to 125-foot tall Astor Column, on top of Coxcomb Hill, provides a fine overview of the surrounding area. An observation deck on top is reached via a spiral staircase, and offers superb views of the city, the four-mile long Astoria-Megler Bridge (the longest continuous truss bridge in the world) across the river to Washington, and the north coast.

The Fort Clatsop National Memorial is operated by the National Park Service to commemorate the Lewis and Clark explorations. The fort was originally built near the mouth of the Columbia River in the autumn of 1805 by a party of 29 adventurers, led by Meriweather Lewis and William Clark. They had just completed one of the most arduous and important explorations in the history of the United States, having crossed the Continental Divide in search of the elusive Northwest Passage to the Pacific Ocean. The original fort has been replaced by an exact replica, following drawings contained in the diaries of the expedition's leaders. In addition to the fort, a visitor center and a busy summer program of frontier skills demonstrations (candle making, tanning, moccasin making, shake-splitting, etc.) make Fort Clatsop Memorial a fascinating place to visit.

Between the Columbia River and Tillamook Head, just south of Seaside, U.S. 101 runs along the Clatsop sand spit. This huge, sandy plain has been built up by sediments carried to the sea by the mighty Columbia River, and then driven up on shore by waves and wind action. Seasonal shifts in prevailing wind direction give rise to beautifully sculpted sand dunes that continuously move across the spit, changing in size and shape. The natural movement of the dunes has been largely halted here, as elsewhere along the coast, by artificial plantings of European beach grass and other non-native plants. The dune stabilization program was begun in the 1930's in an attempt to halt the progression of the dunes across roadways and other structures.

TIDEPOOLS

Rocky areas along the shoreline provide a critical commodity for marine plants and animals - stability. Sandy areas constantly shift back and forth with the currents and tides, and quickly bury or sweep away many potential residents, except those able to burrow into the sand. In contrast, rock outcrops provide the solid home-base needed by a host of marine organisms for part or all of their life cycle. The rocky areas, plus their associated tidepools and channels, that are found between the highest high tides and the lowest low tides comprise the habitat known as the rocky intertidal zone.

Tidepools are fascinating areas for exploration and observation, especially for children. The beauty and diversity of the plants and animals that occupy the rocky intertidal zone captivate the interest and attention of great multitudes of coastal visitors each year. Each species is superbly adapted for conditions in the tidal zone where it occurs, and many of the adaptations are readily apparent to the discerning eye. As the tide recedes, progressively more and more of the unique marine creatures become exposed and are visible to the observant tidepooler.

It is not an easy life, being a tidepool inhabitant. The intertidal environment is very harsh and always changing. Residents are forced to contend with:

· drying out in the air and sunlight when the tide recedes
· continuous battering of waves, especially during severe winter storms
· changes in salinity, especially when it rains at low tide
· problems of oxygen supply, being surrounded by water part of the time and air part of the time in a continuous, alternating cycle
· temperature extremes; marine creatures typically experience a fairly constant temperature under water, whereas the air temperature can drop to below freezing in winter and become very warm in summer.

The various intertidal creatures contend with their difficult and changing environment in a number of interesting ways, including production of biological cement for attachment, suction-cup feet, hard shells, closing up tight to retain moisture, leathery skins, and selection of sites under overhanging ledges or in small crevices that provide protection from the sun, the waves, and the predators. If you have a general feeling for what it must be like to live in a tidepool, and the various adaptations employed by the "locals", your tidepool explorations will be even more interesting and rewarding.

The rocky intertidal community can readily be divided into a number of parallel zones, based upon how often and for how long a period of time the inhabitants are exposed to air versus covered by water. At the top is the spray zone, where residents are frequently splashed by the waves, but are seldom actually submerged. Acorn barnacles, rock snails, and ribbed limpets frequent this zone. Further down is a high tide zone, which is covered by water only twice a day at high tide. Here you can find several kinds of crabs and snails, and the bright green algae

Tillamook Head was formed by a large intrusion of basalt between layers of mudstone and sandstone. Basalt is extremely hard and durable, and withstands well the pounding surf. The softer mudstones and sandstones are much more easily weathered, and uniformly broken down by wind and wave action to form long stretches of smooth coastline, with sandy beaches, between Tillamook Headland and Tillamook Bay. Other small headlands are found along this stretch (Hug Point, Arch Cape, Cape Falcon), and all are the result of basalt flows that resist erosion better than the surrounding mudstones and sandstones. The soft, unstable mudstones are prone to landsliding, evidence of which can be seen at Ecola State Park.

appropriately called sea lettuce. The middle tide zone is covered by water about half of the time, and is home to a rich variety of interesting sea creatures. Beds of gooseneck barnacles and mussels are common. Other typical residents include sea anemones, sponges, limpets, and the common sea star (which comes in purple, orange, and brown variations). The low tide zone is perhaps the most fascinating. Here you have an opportunity to see creatures that are almost always under water. Bright red blood-stars, the huge (up to 2-foot diameter) 24-armed sun-stars, tube worms, ribbon worms, red and purple sea urchins, the giant (up to 12 inches long) gumboot chitons, nudibranchs, sea cucumbers, and sea palms are a few of the local residents. The low tide zone is only accessible to human visitors at minus tides. The lower the tide, the greater the number and diversity of creatures you might find. Be sure to check a tide table (available at fishing tackle shops) before scheduling your tidepool visit.

For best viewing, arrive at the tidepool area an hour or so before low tide during a tidal cycle with negative low-tide values (i.e. lower than average). If you schedule your visit to correspond with a tide that is lower than -2.0, be prepared for some memorable exploring. Tidepool enthusiasts travel great distances to experience a tide of about -2.5 or lower. Remember that many of the creatures uncovered at low tide will be trying to escape the drying of the sun. Look in small crevices and under ledges. Many of the most unusual creatures will only be seen if you really search for them, ever mindful that you must think like a tubeworm if you want to find one!

Please remember that the tidepool environment is extremely fragile and susceptible to disturbance. Be especially careful not to disturb or disrupt the community that lives there. If you pick up or turn over a rock, replace it as you found it. If you move an animal from shade to sunlight, it may not survive long enough to be covered by water again. If you tear off an attached organism, it may be later swept away by the waves and currents. Collection of intertidal plants and animals is prohibited in some tidepool areas, and should be avoided in all tidepool areas. Tidepool observations are best conducted in the intertidal environment, rather than at home!

When exploring tidepools, safety is an important consideration. Be especially careful of four things:

· Algae covered rocks are very slippery.
· A large wave can easily knock you off the rocks. Keep a close eye on the ocean.
· Don't explore alone. As with boating, let someone know when you expect to return.
· When it comes to tides, what goes out must come back in. Many people become stranded on off-shore rocks when the tide returns to the intervening channels. This can be both embarrassing and dangerous.

Enjoy your visit to Oregon's rocky intertidal zone. It is a wonderful place to explore and to catch a glimpse of the rich diversity of Oregon's marine environment.

The small town of Warrenton is a key charter boat center for fishing in the Columbia River. It is also an old fishing village with an unhurried charm, and an artist's or photographer's delight. Fishing activities center on the lower Columbia River and offshore areas, and include salmon, steelhead, and sea-run cutthroat. Another major fishing attraction is the huge sturgeon that are found in this river. The sturgeon fishing is best on the north banks of the river and at Tongue Point, just upriver from Astoria. Anglers fish the river bottom from boats anchored in the deep water, using herring or smelt as bait.

The quiet town of Gearhart is noted for its subdued atmosphere and golf. Gearhart Golf Links, established in 1892, is the oldest course in Oregon. It was designed in a similar fashion to the Scottish links, such as St. Andrews and Dornoch, and covers 100 acres of sand dunes, containing many deep bunkers. The layout is rectangular, one mile long, but only about 500 yards wide. Also nearby is the 9-hole Highlands Golf Course. The beach from 10th Street in Gearhart north to Fort Stevens is open to vehicular traffic, but south of 10th Street the beach is off-limits to motor vehicles and is a more pleasant walking beach.

Seaside, site of the salt-works for the Lewis and Clark expedition, is the major destination resort community of the north coast. Its earlier purpose was to convert seawater to salt in brass kettles. The salt was needed to preserve meat for the expedition's return trip to St. Louis in 1806. Its purpose today is fun and relaxation. The focal point is the Promenade, a broad concrete walkway that parallels the beach for about two miles. It is extremely picturesque and ideal for walking, rollerskating, and bike riding adjacent to the beach. An excellent mixture of history, architecture, shopping and dining complements the beautiful beach and promenade to provide the backdrop for a first class resort community. A plaque to commemorate the official "end" of the Lewis and Clark trail is located at the turn-around where Broadway meets the Promenade. An excellent marine aquarium, public swimming pool, and museum add to the vacation options in Seaside. The visitor's information center is large, well-staffed, and loaded with Oregon Coast travel information. The Seaside Golf Course is situated at the southern end of town, along the Necanicum River. It was built in 1920, and includes a 3,000-year-old Clatsop Indian archaeological site near the 7th hole. It is an easy course, well suited for non-golfing tourists.

Just south of Seaside, the coastline's sandy beaches give way to the state's northernmost headland, Tillamook Head, and one of the most scenic stretches of the Oregon Coast. Ecola State Park covers 1300 acres of rugged coastline between Seaside and Cannon Beach, providing exceptional views of Haystack Rock and south to Neahkahnie Mountain. The view south from Ecola Point is one of the finest on the north coast. The offshore rocks are good places to spot marine birds and sea lions. Whale watching is also good here, for both gray and killer whales. A beautiful six-mile trail leads from Seaside over the headland to Indian Beach, and then continues another six miles along the coast to Cannon Beach. This trail over Tillamook Head is included within the Oregon Coast trail system, and has been designated, with good reason, a National Recreation Trail. The trail climbs 1,100 feet in two miles and includes breath-taking vistas, 1,000-foot cliffs, rain forests, and views of Tillamook Rock, a mile offshore. Use extreme caution if hiking with children.

Tillamook Rock protrudes 90 feet above the sea, with steep walls and an abandoned lighthouse perched on the top. Tillamook Light has withstood the full fury of the Pacific Ocean since 1881. Although it stopped operating as a lighthouse in 1957, it continues to hold its own in its battle with the sea. Today it serves as a depository for cremated human remains. Personally, I preferred it as a lighthouse!

A short 1 1/2 mile detour to the east on Highway 26 from the Cannon Beach Junction will take you to the site of the largest sitka spruce tree in the world. Located just off the north side of the highway, this monstrous spruce is 52 1/2 feet in circumference and 216 feet high. It has been growing here for over 700 years.

Cannon Beach is the cultural capital of the Oregon Coast. Local galleries feature a rich array of art forms. Summer programs are offered in music and the arts; theatrical performances are presented by the Coaster Theater. Named for the cannon that washed ashore when the USS *Shark* sank in 1849, the town is now noted for its art galleries, attractive architecture, and the popular annual Cannon Beach Sandcastle Contest, now in its 27th year, which draws many hundreds of entries each spring. The beach here is wide and beautiful, with a number of picturesque sea stacks offshore. The best known, and most frequently photographed, is the 235-foot-high Haystack Rock. (A second, less famous "Haystack Rock" lies south of Cape Kiwanda, causing some confusion). Haystack Rock is an extremely impressive monolith that dominates the scenery at Cannon Beach. It is also a protected sanctuary for nesting marine birds and intertidal marine life. Western gulls nest here in abundance. Also look for tufted puffins, pelagic cormorants, and pigeon guillemots. Please take note, all you puffin lovers: Haystack Rock is THE place in the lower 48 states to see tufted puffins. About 400 to 500 of these entertaining birds breed here each year. On summer weekends the Haystack Rock Awareness Program and volunteers from the local Puffin Club present interpretive programs. At the base of Haystack Rock are some good tidepools that are well worth exploring at low tide.

WHALE WATCHING

Whale watching has in recent years become an extremely popular pastime on the Oregon coast. Most of the attention has focussed on gray whales, which migrate annually along the Pacific coast between their summer feeding grounds in the Bering Sea and their winter breeding and calving areas in the lagoons of Baja California, in Mexico. Killer whales are also occasionally seen in some of Oregon's coastal bays, but such sightings are relatively rare, and this discussion will therefore focus on the more commonly seen gray whales.

The 12,000-mile annual journey (round trip) of the gray whale is the longest migration of any mammal. Researchers have learned quite a lot about these animals, primarily because they migrate close to shore, where they are easily observed. The southward migration occurs between late November and late January, but peak numbers of whales usually pass along the Oregon coast during the last week in December and first week in January.

The whales travel quickly on the southern leg of their journey; they have important business to attend to in Mexico. The calves are born in the warm waters of the coastal bays and lagoons there, and courtship and breeding activities also occur. The trip back north is more leisurely, and takes place in two pulses. Immature whales of both sexes, the males, and the females that did not give birth to a calf travel north in the first wave of the northward migration in late February and March. In May the cows with calves head north at a much slower rate.

The newborn calves are about 12-15 feet long and weigh up to one ton. They grow another 12 feet or so during the first year, nursing on milk that contains about thirteen times more butterfat than cows milk. Females typically give birth every other year. Over the course of their 60-year lifespan these whales can grow to about 45 feet in length and 45 tons.

Because the whales migrate along the coastline, they can easily be seen from shore, especially from coastal headlands that extend out into the ocean. The animals must detour westward to get around these obstacles and often pass very close to shore. Observations are usually best when the water is calm, particularly in early morning because there is little glare and the winds are often less severe. Look for the spout of vapor that shoots into the air when the animal blows. Once you spot a blow, you will see others in the same vicinity, either from companion whales or from the same animal as it comes to the surface to breathe.

If watching with binoculars from shore only whets your appetite for viewing the whales up-close and personal, you should definitely take a whale-watching charter boat trip. Many of the fishing charter services also offer whale-watching trips during winter, although some require a minimum number of people (often 4-6). Typical costs are about $25 per person for about two hours. Whale-watching is especially popular in Depoe Bay, which bills itself as the whale-watching capital of the world. Viewing the whales right alongside your boat is quite a thrill, especially when the whale is considerably larger than the boat! Close-up viewing is not uncommon. The boat captains are good at finding the whales, which must regularly come to the surface in order to breathe. In addition, the whales themselves are often very curious and will sometimes surface right alongside the boat to do some people-watching.

The Hatfield Marine Science Center operates a program for whale-watching that includes trained volunteers situated at popular whale-watching spots along the coast, including Fort Stevens, Ecola State Park, Neahkahnie Mountain, Cape Meares, Cape Lookout, Boiler Bay, Depoe Bay, Rocky Creek, Cape Foulweather, Devil's Punchbowl, Yaquina Head, Devil's Churn, Cape Perpetua, Sea Lion Caves, Umpqua Lighthouse, Shore Acres, Cape Ferrelo, and Harris Beach State Parks. Call the Marine Science Center for details (867-0246).

One of the nicest beaches on the coast stretches for seven miles southward from Cannon Beach to Arch Cape. It passes by three small points (Silver, Humbug, and Hug Points) which can only be passed at low tide. It is interesting to consider that these beaches have long been used for transportation: as hiking paths for Indians and later as wagon roads for settlers. Headlands and high tides have always caused some degree of difficulty for the traveler. At Hug Point, an old roadbed has been blasted out of the rock. The point received its name because wagons had to hug the headland at low tide and round the point before being caught by the waves. Hug Point State Park offers some interesting exploring along a series of cliffs on the shoreline. The first cliffs to the north are home to a colony of pigeon guillemots. Further north along the beach are found a waterfall and several large caves where you would not like to be stranded at high tide.

Further south, Oswald West State Park stretches along five miles of beautiful coastline, dominated by three rocky headlands: Arch Cape, Cape Falcon, and Neahkahnie Mountain. Named for Oregon's former Governor Oswald West, who is credited with preserving the beaches along most of the state's coastline for public enjoyment, this park offers some of the finest hiking on the coast. Choose your path through lush coastal rain forests, down to Smuggler's Cove, north to Cape Falcon, or along the four-mile trek to the top of 1700-ft-high Neahkahnie Mountain for some of the best views of the coast. Sightings of elk, deer, raccoon, muskrat, and beaver are common. Trailheads can be found at the main parking area 3 1/2 miles south of the Arch Cape Tunnel. Short Sand Beach is one of the most attractive coves on the coast. The nearby campground contains 35 primitive campsites and is for walk-in camping only. The park provides wheelbarrows to help carry campers' gear into the campground, nestled into a quiet spruce forest. Two tide pool areas can be reached from Short Sands Beach, one 1/4 mile to the north, and the other 1/4 mile to the south.

Neahkahnie Mountain, with its often fog-covered summit, has long been known as a "Home of the Gods." South of Neahkahnie Mountain, you can pick up the Coast Trail and hike six miles to Nehalem Bay. If you call a local marina in advance, you can even arrange for ferry service across the bay and then continue your hike down the spit to Nehalem Bay State Park. The bay itself stretches along picturesque, pastoral countryside. Dairy farming and fishing constitute the backbone of the region's economy, although the little town of Manzanita is becoming a popular retirement community. The town of Nehalem is known for its antique shops and sport fishing. Crabbing and clamming are very good, especially in the lower channel for crabs and in the mudflats across the bay from Wheeler for softshell clams. The 100-mile long Nehalem River provides good salmon, steelhead, and trout fishing.

Nehalem Bay State Park extends the length of the four-mile-long Nehalem Bay spit. The park offers a large campground, air strip access 1/4 mile away, and excellent hiking, biking, and horseback riding. There is a nice picnic area at the end of the spit that can be reached on foot or by boat. The horse camp includes 18 stalls for horses, and designated trails are open to horseback riding throughout the park.

Rockaway Beach Wayside provides access to a nice stretch of beach and a view of Twin Rocks, a pair of photogenic sea stacks just off-shore. The southern stack is shaped into a nice arch, the remains of a former cave. Nearby Lake Lytle is popular for swimming, sailing, and waterskiing.

TILLAMOOK BAY TO SILETZ BAY

On the north shore of Tillamook Bay, the little town of Garibaldi is a major center for commercial and sport fishing. Garibaldi has a large fleet of both commercial fishing boats and recreational charter services. Several marinas, boat launches, a good public dock for fishing and crabbing, and access to some fine clamming beds round out the major opportunities in this community that revolves around fishing activities. Nearby Barview County Park, on the north bank of the mouth of Tillamook Bay, provides access to a nice walking beach, excellent jetty fishing, and a campground. The north jetty provides a great opportunity for observing pelagic bird species. The bay outlet is good for grebes, loons, and bay ducks, and is also a good place to see harbor seals and sea lions.

Tillamook Bay offers some of the best clamming on the coast, good crabbing off the Bayocean Peninsula and the old Garibaldi Coast Guard Pier, great fall salmon fishing, and spectacular concentrations of waterfowl. During fall and winter, Tillamook Bay is one of the best birding areas on the coast. Shorebirds and waterfowl are abundant. The breeding colonies of tufted puffins and great blue herons here are among the largest in Oregon. Bald eagles nest nearby, and killer whales can sometimes be spotted in the bay during spring. In addition, five top-quality salmon/steelhead rivers empty into the bay: the Miami, Kilchis, Trask, Wilson, and Tillamook Rivers. Boat launch areas are abundant.

Tillamook itself is home to the largest tourist attraction on the Oregon coast. The Tillamook Creamery hosts 800,000 visitors per year. They come to see how Tillamook cheddar cheese is made - some 30 million pounds each year, although the fresh-made ice cream is also a popular feature. Other attractions in Tillamook include the Pioneer Museum, Navy blimp hangars, and scenic railroad trips. Tillamook is a dairy-farming community and the cows clearly outnumber the human population. The Alderbrook golf course, located north of town, is built on flat pasture land and is easy to walk. Water hazards are frequent.

Tillamook County Pioneer Museum, located downtown in the old (1905) courthouse, contains three floors of exceptional exhibits and over 35,000 artifacts, ranging from stagecoaches, canoes, and nautical equipment to antique cameras, toys and Indian baskets. The museum also contains good natural history exhibits and a huge wildlife collection. It is a great stop on a rainy day.

A few miles south of town are the U.S. Navy blimp hangars, built during WW II to house a fleet of surveillance blimps that patrolled the coastline. Reputed to be the largest open-span wooden buildings in the world, the hangars are 1,000 feet long and 170 feet high. Be sure to sneak a peak inside through one of the windows or open crevices. They are far more impressive on the inside. Now property of the Port of Tillamook, these monstrous structures are largely unused, but do house some businesses and sometimes contain a drug patrol blimp.

The Oregon Coastline Express, which began service in 1989, can be boarded at the train station on 3rd Street for a scenic train trip along the bay and north to Garibaldi, Rockaway Beach, and Wheeler. This popular trip offers superb views of the coast and its wildlife resources. The 25-mile trip to Wheeler takes about 2 hours (for information call 842-2768). The season begins March 1.

South of Tillamook is a county park at Munsen Creek Falls, the highest waterfalls in the Coast Range (266 feet). Two trails lead from a parking area to the falls. The upper trail has very steep drop-offs and is not recommended for small children, although the view from the top is well worth the hike.

Bayocean Peninsula is a narrow spit of sand that separates Tillamook Bay from the Pacific Ocean. The road along the spit can be driven for about a mile, and then you can hike out the peninsula for some excellent birding and access to first-rate clamming beds. The three-mile hike, or bike ride, out along the sandspit offers a tremendous diversity of bird species in an incredible variety of habitats: grassland, coniferous forest, dune, marsh, scotch broom fields, bay, mudflats, and sand beach. The ill-fated resort community of Bayocean was once located here and contained 59 houses, a three-story hotel, and a large natatorium, a 160-foot long indoor salt water swimming pool. In the 1930s and 1940s, many of the buildings were destroyed in a series of storms by the encroaching ocean. By 1952, the southern end of the spit was eroded away to the point that the ocean broke through directly to the bay, and the remainder of the spit became an island. The buildings continued to fall to the powerful waves, and the last of the residents finally deserted what was left of the town. After the south jetty was completed in 1965, the near-shore currents and sand deposition patterns were changed, and the spit was gradually rebuilt by the sea. Not a trace remains today of the former resort town.

Southwest of Tillamook, a beautiful 20-mile loop passes along some spectacular headland scenery past Cape Meares and Netarts. Rather than returning directly to Tillamook, a popular option is to continue driving south along the Three Capes Scenic Drive. This 65-mile loop includes Capes Lookout and Kiwanda, in addition to Cape Meares. Avid birders may see over 75 species in a day's birding along Tillamook Bay and around the loop.

Cape Meares State Park is an enjoyable stop, having a lighthouse, exceptional views of the coastline and off-shore rocks, whale watching, birding, and the popular "octopus tree". This enormous sitka spruce tree branches out into six candelabra limbs that each grow out horizontally for 20 or 30 feet and then turn upwards, resembling an upside-down octopus. Cape Meares State Park and National Wildlife Refuge contain good concentrations of seals and sea lions, as well as nesting murres, cormorants, and tufted puffins, particularly on the islands off-shore. The best views of the marine mammals and birds are afforded along the short trail between the parking lot and lighthouse.

Netarts Bay is too shallow to provide much of a fin fishery, but crabbing and clamming are excellent here. The best clamming is off the spit, where cockles, butter, gaper, and littleneck clams are all abundant. The bay is generally good for family boating, although the bar can be quite dangerous. Birding is good, especially at high tide, for waterfowl and shorebirds. In late summer, the bay is frequented by brown pelicans.

Cape Lookout is a long, narrow basaltic headland with very steep sides that extends two miles out to sea. It is a beautiful and rugged headland that contains a lush rain forest and large colonies of sea birds that nest on the cliffs and offshore sea stacks. A 2 1/2 mile trail leads to the end of the headland and offers some exceptional hiking, with great views, magnificent sitka spruce forests, and steep cliffs. (Exercise caution with small children.) The sights may include whales, sea lions, and bald eagles. Cape Lookout State Park encompasses not only the cape itself, but also the beaches to the north up to the mouth of Netarts Bay. A popular campground and picnic area provide access to a great beach.

Cape Kiwanda, the last of the "three capes", is a small and attractive headland of sandstone. Haystack Rock is just offshore (not to be confused with

WILDLIFE

Opportunities for wildlife-viewing at the coast are many and varied. The great diversity of coastal habitat types (ocean, bay, beach, mudflat, rain forest, dunes, fresh water, etc.) provides homes for an enormous variety of wildlife. Two extremely popular wildlife-viewing activities that are discussed as separate issues in other inset boxes in this book are tidepooling and whale watching. Other popular viewing activities are centered upon seals and sea lions, birds, and elk, each of which is discussed below. In addition, the observant visitor may encounter, at many places along the coastline, one of any number of fascinating wildlife species; these include black bear, rabbit, otter, deer, bobcat, and coyote, among others. Early morning hours are most likely to be successful.

A string of 1400 islands off the Oregon coast comprise the Oregon Islands National Wildlife Refuge. These largely basaltic rock outcrops are home to colonies of seabirds and marine mammals. Many of these can be viewed from the mainland, especially with binoculars or spotting scope. Good mainland viewing sites include Cape Meares, Cape Lookout, Cape Kiwanda, Yaquina Head, Boardman State Park, and Brookings. Some charter boat operators will also take visitors out to the off-shore rocks for closer viewing. Note, however, that boats should not venture within 200 yards of the islands included within the wildlife refuge. It is illegal to cause the birds to leave their nests.

Three Arch Rocks National Wildlife Refuge and Cape Meares National Wildlife Refuge are both located west of Tillamook. The former is the site of Oregon's largest seabird colony. The three main rocks and six smaller ones are home to about 200,000 nesting common murres, plus assorted other species, including tufted puffins, storm petrels, and cormorants. The Cape Meares Refuge is located on the mainland, and includes 138 acres of old growth sitka spruce and western hemlock forest. Vertical sea cliffs provide nesting habitat for several species of marine birds.

The fourth and final national wildlife refuge on the Oregon Coast is Bandon Marsh. It includes 289 acres of salt marsh at the mouth of the Coquille River. This is one of the few remaining natural salt marshes on the coast, and is home to a great diversity of bird life. It provides important wintering habitat for shorebirds and waterfowl.

Steller sea lions and harbor seals are the most common pinnipeds seen in Oregon, although elephant seals are also occasionally encountered. The sea lions differ from seals in that they have limbs that can be turned inward to help them walk on land; in contrast seals must drag themselves laboriously along the ground some-the other Haystack Rock at Cannon Beach). The sandstone cliffs give rise to very large sand dunes that are extremely popular for hang gliding. Cape Kiwanda is reputed to be one of the safest places on the Oregon coast to learn and practice this sport. Hang gliding enthusiasts from all over the Pacific Northwest come here, beginning in May when the wind pattern shifts to northwesterly.

Some of the best surfing on the Oregon Coast can be found on the south side of the cape. Be forewarned, however, that in recent years several Oregon surfers have had encounters with great white sharks. The surfers generally come out the losers. Apparently, a surfboard looks somewhat like the underside of a seal if you are a shark looking upward. The large increase in the state's seal populations in the past two decades may have drawn more great whites from southern waters. Or maybe the sharks were always here, but previously had fewer surfers to choose from!

The major area on the north coast for dunebuggies is around Sand Lake, north of Cape Kiwanda. South of the cape, Pacific City provides some choice photo opportunities. It is a small fishing

what resembling giant slugs. Another point of distinction is that sea lions have visible external ears (located on the sides of their heads, of course!), whereas most seals do not. Marked on the sectional maps are the principal locations for viewing seals and sea lions. These are most often haul-out areas where the animals lie on the beach or rocks to bask in the sun.

There are many places along the coast to observe colonies of nesting sea birds, in some cases on the off-shore islands of the Oregon Islands National Wildlife Refuge, and in other cases on rocky cliffs along the mainland. Murres, tufted puffins, three species of cormorants, auklets, murrelets, and several species of gulls comprise most of the resident species. Nesting sites are typically occupied from April through August. Some of the largest colonies contain up to a hundred thousand individuals. Please do not disturb the nesting birds, and stay at least 500 feet from the nest sites. Human disturbance is an enormous problem and can cause devastation of the nesting areas. Eggs or young are often knocked off the cliffs or rocks when the adult birds are frightened; deserted nests are also far more susceptible to predators, such as gulls.

There are good places for birding virtually everywhere along the coast. Some of the more noteworthy areas are marked on the maps. All you need is a pair of binoculars, a field guide, and a small dose of persistence, and you will see a great many bird species. Some of the more popular ones include bald eagles, ospreys, and great blue herons. These three are attracted to water because of their preference for fish in their diets. The alert visitor is almost guaranteed to be rewarded with at least one unusual sighting.

Although elk can be seen at any number of places along the coast, you are almost guaranteed to see these magnificent animals at the Bureau of Land Management's Dean Creek Elk Viewing Area, just east of Reedsport on Highway 38. A large herd makes its home on this former ranch. The elk are often very close to the road and developed parking areas, and binoculars are not needed. This is a great place to get a close-up picture of elk in their natural habitat, without the benefit of a huge telephoto lens. Use care when parking along the highway. Traffic is moderately high and includes many log and freight trucks traveling at high speeds.

Please recognize that coastal animals are, and should be, wild. They should not be treated as pets. Please view from a distance to minimize disturbance, and do not attempt to feed wildlife. Watching from a distance not only allows you to observe the natural behavior of the animals, it is also far more rewarding. While many people have good intentions of helping animals they think are stranded, their efforts to capture and care for the animal are often more stressful and damaging to it than leaving the animal undisturbed. Animals that appear to be injured or stranded should be reported to the Oregon Department of Fish and Wildlife, but left alone.

town without a harbor. The beach here is long and gently sloped. Commercial fishermen drive on the hard-packed sand and launch their fishing dories directly into the surf. The entire exercise is quite fascinating, and watching the launching of the Pacific Dory Fleet in the early morning light has become a popular tourist activity.

Hikers can proceed eight miles along the beaches from Sand Lake to the mouth of Nestucca Bay. Along the way, the trail detours over the top of Cape Kiwanda. The bay can be crossed by boat if prior arrangements are made (Nestucca Marina in Pacific City, 964-6410). Nestucca Bay yields some of the largest catches of salmon and steelhead on the Oregon Coast, over 5,000 of each in some years. The bay is also good for clamming, especially on the east side for softshells. Between the south end of the mouth of Nestucca Bay and Neskowin is a five-mile stretch of beautiful beach that is very remote from civilization. Neskowin is a relaxing little village, best known for its golf and its quaint atmosphere. Neskowin Beach Golf Course, built in 1932, contains frequent water hazards, but no traps. Located six feet above sea level, the course floods during much of the winter. On the opposite side of the coast highway is Hawk Creek Golf Course. It is peaceful and secluded, and is often visited by wildlife, including deer, bear, and elk.

Cascade Head is a rugged headland, covered primarily by coastal rain forest, that rises to an elevation of 1770 feet. It contains a rich variety of wildlife and provides excellent hiking opportunities. Part of the area is preserved as a Scenic-Research Area managed by Siuslaw National Forest. A Nature Conservancy trail leads to a grassy knoll 1000 feet above the sea. The views and whale watching here are great. Cascade Head is unusual among the coastal headlands for the extent of its grassland, dominated by native grasses and herbaceous plants. Indian paintbrush, goldenrod, blue violet, and lupine provide splashes of color to this picturesque and pristine area. Two rare plant species, the Cascade Head catchfly and the hairy checkermallow, and one rare insect species, the Oregon silverspot butterfly, are found only at Cascade Head and a few other spots. Bald eagles, marsh hawks, red-tailed hawks, and occasionally peregrine falcons hunt the grassy slopes. Black-tailed deer, great horned owls, coyotes, and snowshoe hares occupy the forests and forest edge. The nearby Sitka Center for Art and Ecology is an excellent wildlife viewing area, where bald eagles, hawks, and deer are common. The center offers classes in art, photography, and ecology for all age groups, as well as a number of special events.

Lincoln City, formed by the merger of five coastal towns, is a bustling strip of tourist shops and motels, and has a large factory-outlet shopping center and an attractive golf course. It also has access to some beautiful beaches and two-mile long Devil's Lake. This warm water lake is popular for camping, canoeing, swimming, and fishing. It contains good populations of bass, yellow perch, and brown bullhead. Grass carp, an exotic species of fish, have been introduced experimentally in an attempt to control the excessive growth of aquatic weeds. To celebrate the improved water quality, residents hold the annual Grass Carp festival in September. Lacey's Doll House Museum, 3400 NE Highway 101, displays over 2,000 dolls from all over the world, including a wooden doll made in 1740.

A nice stretch of beach extends the length of Lincoln City from Roads End to Siletz Bay. There are numerous access points, most notably "D" River Wayside and Roads End Wayside. The "D" River is listed in the Guiness Book of World Records as the shortest river in the world, and flows from the outlet of Devil's Lake to the ocean for the distance of about one eleven-year-old right-fielder's throwing range. The beach at "D" Sands is one of the most popular on the coast for kite flying. Horse enthusiasts will enjoy the annual Driftwood Derby, which includes a number of horse racing events. The triatholon event is popular, and involves canoeing across Devil's Lake, bicycling 2 1/2 miles, and horseback riding 2 miles on the beach.

Upper Drift Creek covered bridge is southeast of Lincoln City. Built in 1914 for about $1,800, the bridge is now only open to foot traffic and is preserved as an historical memorial. It is Oregon's oldest remaining covered bridge.

Siletz Bay is popular for windsurfing and crabbing. Seals, loons, grebes, and brown pelicans can often be seen in the bay. A good observation point can be found at Siletz Bay Park, just north of Schooner Creek in the Taft area. Bald eagles frequent the bay area and nest near Devil's Lake. The Siletz River is one of the best steelhead rivers in the state, and is also excellent for salmon and trout. On the southern end of the bay is found the famous Salishan Resort, complete with a first-rate golf course, indoor pool and tennis courts, shopping mall, first-

BEACH SAFETY

The Oregon Coast is a fascinating and delightful playground for recreationists. It is also a rugged expanse of coastline exposed to the full fury of the Pacific Ocean. While the Pacific can delight all of the senses, it also can and does kill many unwary visitors. This ocean demands a great deal of respect, and you would be ill-advised to take it lightly.

The principal coastal safety concerns are listed below. Each of these issues warrants careful consideration on the part of the coastal recreationist.

· **Rocks and cliffs** - Presumably everyone is aware of the dangers associated with hiking along cliff edges and climbing or scrambling over rocks at the coastline. It is best to stick to marked trails, and be especially cautious when young children are present. A less frequently recognized danger involves the interactions between coastal rocks and cliffs and the changing tidal cycle. A short hop across a narrow channel to access an interesting rock in the intertidal zone can quickly leave you facing an impassible, wide, and churning tidal channel as the tide comes in. Many visitors each year become stranded by the tide on off-shore rocks. Similarly, a hike along the cliffs on a wide beach at low tide can leave the unwary hiker stranded between the cliffs and the surf as the tide quickly returns to the cliff base. Be especially careful when hiking past small promontories or headland areas at low tide; you may have to wait on the other side until the tide goes back out again, many hours later.

· **Sneaker waves** - A wave that is much larger than others in the series is called a "sneaker" wave. It washes high onto the beach and can be quite dangerous, as all-too-often someone is swept from the shoreline out to sea by one of these sneakers. They are particularly dangerous at jetties and rocky areas. Always keep one eye on the ocean, and be prepared to move yourself, and your children, higher up the beach on fairly short notice.

· **Logs** - Many beaches on the Oregon coast are littered with large logs that have washed up onto the shore. Stay clear of any logs you might see in the water or at the water's edge. They float easily when the water washes in, and quickly crush anything that happens to end up beneath them when the water rushes out.

· **Riptides and undertows** - Only the most hardy will swim at the Oregon coast. Except for a few sheltered coves, the water never warms sufficiently for normal people to stay in more than a few minutes. Remember that the water here is too cold to survive in it for a long period of time, and consequently riptides and undertows can be doubly dangerous. First, it may be difficult to swim back to shore, and second, you will not have too much time to get out of the water. Swim on in-coming tides when the dangers of riptides are lessened. If you are caught in a riptide, swim parallel to shore in order to get out of it. Never try to swim directly against a riptide; you can't.

Hikers should exercise particular caution at the coast. Never hike very far without adequate clothing (including rain gear), matches, sunglasses, drinking water, extra clothes, first aid kit, map, compass, and a flashlight with extra batteries. The latter several items may be needed if you must leave the beach and hike inland to reach a road. Be particularly careful in southern Oregon, because the highway is remote from the coastline in many places and the landscape is very rugged. Coastal streams more than knee-deep should not be crossed. Stream depth fluctuates widely in response to weather conditions, season, and tidal cycles. Frequently, it is easy to detour around a difficult stream crossing by hiking inland to a road.

It is hard to imagine a nicer place to vacation than the Oregon coast. But please exercise caution, and you will return home with only pleasant memories.

class restaurant, conference facilities, and all of the other amenities of a major destination resort. Salishan Golf Links is one of the best in Oregon. The front nine is wooded and hilly; the back nine features narrow, windswept fairways with Scottish-type bunkers and superb views out over Siletz Bay.

DEPOE BAY TO CAPE PERPETUA

Boiler Bay State Park, a mile north of Depoe Bay, provides access to some good tidepools, whale watching, and excellent birding opportunities. Many unusual bird sightings are recorded here. The bay was named for the boiler of the steam schooner *J. Marhoffer* that burned offshore and beached here in 1910. The boiler is still visible in the water at low tide, although the rest of the vessel has long-since been consumed by the sea.

Depoe Bay features the "smallest harbor in the world" and an extremely narrow (50 ft) channel to the ocean through which scores of fishing boats pass each day on their way to the superb offshore fishing grounds. There are nearly 50,000 ocean fishing trips out of this tiny (6 acre) harbor each year, and the success ratio is generally as high as anywhere on the Coast. It is hard to imagine a better place to hop on an ocean charter boat and go after a chinook or coho salmon. Whale watching boat trips here are also quite popular. The picturesque little bay was the site of Jack Nicholson's (a.k.a. Randall McMurphy) hijacking of a charter boat along with a boatload of other asylum inmates in the film *One Flew Over the Cuckoo's Nest*.

Winter storms sometimes send spouts of water flying across the highway in town, as huge waves crash against the rocks below. The observation deck on the north side of the Depoe Bay Bridge is a good spot to watch the surf and the boating activities. Visit the State Park building there to see the interpretive exhibits in the top floor viewing area.

South of Depoe Bay, the short Otter Crest Loop Road hugs the rugged coastline of Cape Foulweather, and offers some great vistas. At the outer end is found Devil's Punchbowl, a collapsed sea cave; it resembles a giant pot that churns and boils with seawater at high tide.

Newport, on the banks of Yaquina Bay, is one of the largest cities on the Oregon Coast. It is multifaceted, being very much a resort town, yet retaining the flavor of a busy, working fishing port. The Bay Front is the most interesting part of town. It has canneries, commercial fishing boats, and charter services interspersed with restaurants, shops and tourist attractions. The Wax Museum, Ripley's Believe-it-or-Not, and Undersea Gardens provide the touristy touch; a public wharf next to a busy fishing boat dock provides the salty charm; and Mo's Annex provides some of the best clam chowder anywhere. The Lincoln County Historical Museum and "haunted" Yaquina Bay Lighthouse in Yaquina Bay State Park are worthwhile stops. From the park, you have a good vantage point for photographing the fishing boats as they cross beneath the attractive Yaquina Bay Bridge, on their way to and from the offshore fishing grounds.

Newport is very popular as a destination resort town and fishing center, and offers a tremendous diversity of things to see and do. The wharf on the Bay Front provides a good vantage point for watching the fishing boats in the bay and the antics of the ubiquitous seals and sea lions near shore. Once or twice a year, during spring, small pods of killer whales venture into the bay to dine on the seals or sea lions. Across the bay at South Beach can be found the Hatfield Marine Science Center, a large marina and public dock, some good birdwatching, clamming beds, and the Oregon Aquarium (scheduled to open in 1992).

The Hatfield Marine Science Center, a research station of Oregon State University, has an excellent (and free-of-charge) aquarium, whale skeletons, bird specimens, an octopus tank, and a children's touch tank full of intertidal creatures such as sea urchins, starfish, limpets, and the like. The films, educational programs, exhibits, and natural history bookstore are all very good, and it is not surprising that nearly a half-million visitors stop here each year.

As one of the most productive sport fishing ports on the coast, Newport has a large fleet of charter fishing boats. Fishing offshore is excellent for bottom fish, salmon, and far offshore for halibut and tuna. Fishing is also very good from the public dock at the Newport Marina at South Beach, both jetties, and in the surf at South Beach. Newport is also one of the more popular harbors for whale watching charters.

Yaquina Head Lighthouse (not to be confused with Yaquina Bay Lighthouse, located on the north bank of the bay), situated just north of Newport within the Yaquina Head Outstanding Natural Area, commands a good view of the coastline, and is very

BOATING SAFETY TIPS

· Wear your life jacket, especially in a small boat. Most people who drown in boating accidents are not wearing a life jacket; most would have survived had they been wearing one
· Boating and alcohol do not mix
· Carry a fire extinguisher aboard your motorboat
· Check weather forecasts and pay attention to changing weather conditions
· Know about cold water survival
· Do not overload your boat
· Distribute weight evenly
· Watch your wake and be courteous to others on the water
· Tell someone where you are going and when you will return
· For questions regarding boating safety, boating regulations, or law enforcement, contact your local County Sheriff's office or the State Marine Board

popular for tidepooling, birdwatching, and whale watching. The lighthouse is not open to the public; it has been automated and is still an operating guide to navigation. The Outstanding Natural Area encompasses 100 acres of the headland, and is managed as a natural preserve by the Bureau of Land Management. It is a day-use area, open from dawn to dusk, and is staffed by rangers throughout the day. The tidepools have been designated a Marine Garden by the Oregon Department of Fish and Wildlife, and collecting intertidal organisms is not permitted.

The observation deck behind the Yaquina Head Lighthouse affords good views of the nesting seabirds on the offshore rock, and is an excellent whale watching viewpoint. The harbor seal haul-out rock is visible from the landings on the stairway down to the tidepools. Harbor seals can be seen here at close range year-round.

The offshore rocks and cliffs at Yaquina Head support large populations of nesting marine birds, mostly common murres and Brandt's cormorants. There is also a good diversity of gulls, and a group of tufted puffins nest on the northwest side of the main offshore rock. Yaquina Bay itself also provides several good birding options. Yaquina Bay State Park is good for songbirds. Idaho Flats is one of the best places on the coast for shorebirds, especially as the tide starts to go out. The South Jetty is great for bay ducks, loons, grebes, and scoters.

The Mike Miller Park Educational Trail, just south of the Yaquina Bay Bridge, is a 45-minute self-guided hike through a coastal sitka spruce forest. Numbered posts along the trail correspond to information provided by a brochure distributed by Lincoln County (880 N.E. 7th Street, Newport 97365). Beach hiking is excellent from South Beach southward, all the way to Yachats. The only detours are around the small headland at Seal Rock, across the Alsea Bay Bridge at Waldport, and a short stretch along Highway 101 coming into Yachats.

Waldport, on the south bank of the lower Alsea River, provides access to some nice walking beaches and good clamming beds. It is one of the premier bays on the coast for Dungeness crabs. The river is excellent for sea-run cutthroat, coho, and chinook salmon. Just north of the bay in some old-growth trees is a bald eagle nesting area that has been highly productive for at least the last 25 years. Alsea Bay provides good birding at Lint Slough, and particularly one mile further east at Eckman Slough. The road that heads south up Eckman Slough (just past the causeway that crosses over the slough along Highway 34) is a good place for waterfowl in winter and during migrations.

The Drift Creek Wilderness, managed by the U.S. Forest Service, is a nine-square-mile preserve of steep ridges, remote streams, forests, and meadows northeast of Waldport. The area contains some of the largest remaining stands of old-growth coastal rain forests. It is accessible only by trail. Contact the Waldport Ranger Station for specifics.

Starting between Waldport and Yachats and then extending south past Heceta (Ha SEE ta) Head is a large stretch of basalt that creates a gorgeous rocky coastline of headlands and small sandy coves. The basalt is from 50-million year old, underwater lava flows that have been broken and fragmented by the intense wave action.

The tiny town of Yachats (YAH-hots) is nestled between a very rugged stretch of basaltic coastline and the Coast Range Mountains. It is one of the best towns on the coast for storm-watching. A major attraction is the netting of silver smelt that spawn in the sands of Yachats Beach each spring. Locals catch their limit using dip nets, providing a fun

BICYCLING

Bicycling has in recent years become extremely popular on the Oregon coast. The State has designated a coastal bike route, which follows Highway 101 in most places, with some alternative detours, for example around the Three Capes Scenic Drive southwest of Tillamook, the Otter Crest Loop south of Depoe Bay, and Seven Devils Road north of Bandon. Contact the Oregon Department of Parks and Recreation or Oregon Department of Transportation for maps and details.

Because most coastal biking is done in the summer months, and the prevailing wind direction in summer is from north to south, the highly intelligent bicyclist will ride from north to south also. The not-so-intelligent bicyclist will ride a short distance from south to north and then will probably end up on a bus with his or her bike, because it is generally quite windy on the coast and a strong headwind will spoil your trip!

Some sections of the coast bike route have wide shoulders, perfectly suited for leisurely bike travel. Other sections are narrow, winding, and a bit frightening as those giant RVs and logging trucks go whizzing by your left ear. Use particular caution when riding off Highway 101 on the loop roads. Make your bicycle as visible as possible (e.g., with bright clothing and touring bags and a fluorescent fanny triangle), and ride as far to the right side as possible.

A large number of campgrounds in Oregon have hiker/biker campsites. These are reserved for use by travelers using non-motorized forms of transportation; that means bikes. Generally, you can camp at these sites for up to two nights for a modest fee.

In addition to the coast bike route, which is primarily suited to the serious biker, there are also paved bicycle trails available in two of the state parks. These are excellent for family biking and provide a nice way to see the countryside away from the noisy roadways. Fort Stevens State Park contains nine miles of bike trails that wind throughout the park. Nehalem Bay State Park has 1 1/2 miles of paved bike trails that intertwine with an extensive network of equestrian trails.

Mountain biking enthusiasts will find an abundance of gravel and dirt roads on U.S. Forest Service and Bureau of Land Management lands adjoining Highway 101. These roads were developed to provide logging access. They create a maze of bicycling opportunities through scenic forest stands, up and down sometimes extremely steep grades, and along ridge-tops and streams. Detailed maps of the road systems can be obtained at BLM and Forest Service offices.

---

spectacle for tourists and photographers. Bird watchers may want to see the marbled murrelets fly up and down the river at dawn and dusk. Small tidepool areas are scattered along the shoreline for about 1/2 mile north of the Yachats River.

Strawberry Hill, three miles south of Yachats in Neptune State Park, is a turnout along Highway 101 that overlooks huge rocks just offshore that are home to a large number of harbor seals. They are easily photographed across a 30-yard channel. Also accessible are some nice tidepools and a variety of sea birds.

CAPE PERPETUA TO CAPE ARAGO

Cape Perpetua is a prominent basaltic headland, on which the narrow Highway 101 snakes along shoreline cliffs. The Siuslaw National Forest operates the Cape Perpetua Visitor Center, which features exhibits, films, and access to a number of popular attractions. Trails lead up into the Coast Range forests, to a giant spruce tree, historic Indian middens (shell mounds), Devil's Churn, and a spectacular overlook area. Devil's Churn is a narrow fissure in the basaltic cliffs along the water's edge. At high tide, waves rush through the chasm and erupt into the air with a mighty splash. The overlook, at an elevation of 800 feet, can be reached by trail or road from the visitor's center. It is an excellent location for hiking, whale watching, or photography, with views on a clear day from Cape Foulweather to Cape Blanco and 30 or 40 miles out to sea. The Gwynn Creek Trail can be accessed via a portion of the Oregon Coast Trail from the Cape Perpetua Visitor's Center. It provides a pleasant 6 1/2 mile loop through lush old-growth Douglas fir and sitka spruce forests. A self-guided auto tour through the coastal forest departs from Highway 101 just north of the Visitor's Center and returns to the coast at Yachats.

Heceta Head, named for the Spanish navigator Bruno Heceta, is graced by the most picturesque and most photographed lighthouse on the Oregon coast. The 1893-vintage white tower with red-tile roof, and nearby Victorian keeper's house, provide a photographer's dream, especially in the early morning light looking north. Nearby Devil's Elbow State Park offers a very nice beach for surf fishing, great views of the adjacent picturesque bridge and coastline to the south, and also excellent whale watching.

Further south is found Sea Lion Caves, a very popular tourist attraction that features the only permanent colony of Steller sea lions on the U.S. mainland. An enormous sea cave, with 125-foot high ceilings, is host to hundreds of these marine mammals. An admission fee will allow you to descend into the cave via elevator, along with 200,000 other visitors each year. The adjacent cliffs provide nesting sites for all three of Oregon's cormorant species, as well as pigeon guillemots.

Darlingtonia Botanical Wayside has a short loop trail through a pleasant wooded park that contains the rare cobra lilies, also known as pitcher plants. These carnivorous plants make up for a nitrogen-deficient environment by luring insect prey into a tube lined with sweet nectar, a tube from which these hapless creatures will never return! Raised walkways wind through the marshy botanical preserve that contains many of these large plants with hooded leaves that resemble cobra snakes.

Eight miles north of Florence begins a stretch of sandy coastline derived from sedimentary rocks. This is the northern extent of the spectacular Oregon dunes country, which continues south to Coos Bay. The sand is produced by the breakdown of the local sedimentary rocks, which contain a great deal of sand, and by sand carried to the ocean by local rivers. The sand is brought onto the beach by wave action, then dries and is blown inland by the prevailing winds. Winds tend to be from the southwest in winter and from the northwest in summer, and the dunes change in shape and character in response to the continuous onslaught of the winds. Active sand dunes gradually bury forests in some sections of this portion of coastline, eventually killing the trees and leaving dead tree trunks protruding from the dunes. Many lakes are found in the dunes country, having been formed by sand deposits blocking the flow of coastal streams. The water in these lakes generally exits by underground seepage into the sand, rather than stream flow to the sea.

One of the coast's most popular vacation spots, Florence offers a rich history tied to logging and fishing. Situated on the banks of the Siuslaw River, it is the gateway to the vast Oregon Dunes National Recreation Area, as well as a good base for accessing a myriad of excellent lake, river, and ocean fishing opportunities. Old Town, on the north bank, has been largely renovated and is the most visited portion of Florence. The city's annual Rhododendron Festival in May has been held for over 75 years. It attracts thousands of visitors each year for a wide range of family entertainment. The bay provides good clamming, especially for softshells, and good crabbing off the concrete pier near the south jetty. Both the bay and lower river provide good fishing for sea-run cutthroat, salmon, and steelhead. The south jetty provides views of the seals and sea lions that frequent the lower river. The marsh lands to the south of the jetty are home to a flock of swans in winter.

North of Florence, C&M Stables offers fabulous horseback riding along vast stretches of beach. South of town lies Siltcoos Lake, the largest of Oregon's coastal lakes. It provides very good sport fishing for virtually every sport fish species that occur in Oregon freshwaters. Native cutthroat, rainbow trout, and coho fishing can be very good. Siltcoos Lake is also considered one of the best warm-water fishing lakes in the state. The warm-water quarry range from trophy size bass (8 pounds plus) to plentiful yellow perch and bluegill. There are six primitive hiker/boater camps on the lakeshore. A two-mile trail leads from the Siltcoos Lake Trailhead, located eight miles south of Florence, through coastal forest to the lake. Rewards of the hike are peace, solitude, and beautiful lakeside scenery.

The Oregon Dunes National Recreation Area (ODNRA) is an enormous 45-mile long sand dune area that boasts the highest dunes in the United States (some over 500 feet) and a wealth of recreational opportunities. About half of the ODNRA is off-limits to motor vehicles and provides some excellent hiking; the other half is an unsurpassed playground for dune-buggy and three-wheeler enthusiasts. Hikers are well-advised to stick to the non-motorized half. A string of freshwater lakes lies just inland of the major dune systems, and provides great warm-water fishing, canoeing, and swimming. At Cleawox Lake, a 100-foot sand dune slopes directly into the water, providing a natural slide for swimmers. Campgrounds abound, and are operated by the U.S. Forest Service, State, County, and private individuals, providing a total of about 2000 campsites. Honeyman State Park is extremely popular, and with good reason. The excellent swimming, boating, hiking, and fishing in the park, combined with forests, enormous dunes, sandy beach on Cleawox Lake, attractive campground and picnic facilities, create a vacation paradise. Dunes City has a commercial dune buggy operation. The off-road-vehicle (ORV) enthusiasts tend to congregate around the Siltcoos River Recreation Area, the area to the south of South Jetty Road, south of Umpqua Lighthouse State Park, and north of Horsfall Road. Maps and regulations for ORV users are available at the ODNRA office in Reedsport.

Popular Tahkenitch Lake is a good place to see bald eagles and ospreys. Its many arms and extensive shoreline provide plenty of territory to explore by canoe.

Nearly 250 species of birds, including bald eagles and ospreys, can be seen in the ODNRA. Several hundred white tundra swans winter on the shallow lakes about five miles south of Florence. The marshy lakes are east of South Jetty Road, and the birds can be easily seen from the road with binoculars. A hike along the trail from Waxmyrtle Campground to an overlook above the Siltcoos Estuary is likely to afford a glimpse of a bald eagle, found here year-round.

Forty-five miles of open beach in the ODNRA are accessible to horseback riders. Hang gliders have ample opportunity to pursue their sport. And despite the area's popularity, peace and solitude can be found in the more remote sections of the non-motorized half of the ODNRA.

The Overlook, 10 miles north of Reedsport, offers views of the dunes country from three levels of viewing decks. Birding, including ospreys, is good here. Deer and bear are sometimes sighted. A one-mile trail leads through the dunes to the ocean. When visiting the dunes, be aware that these fascinating structures would not exist were it not for the nearly constant off-shore winds. It is therefore advisable to carry a windbreaker. Also, small children have the misfortune of having their eyes located two or three feet off the ground, which also happens to be where most of the sand is blowing. Be prepared to carry "Junior".

The Umpqua River flows into the sea through the middle of the dunes country. Reedsport, on the south bank, is the tourism center for this area and contains the ODNRA Headquarters and Visitor Center. The Umpqua River was once an important transportation corridor between the Willamette Valley and the coast. It is now one of the state's prime recreation rivers. Some of the largest beaches in Oregon extend both north and south of the mouth of the river. Inland scenery is spectacular. The Umpqua is a large river with a superb salmon fishery. It is renowned for its spring chinook runs. Shad fishing in spring and summer, sturgeon fishing in the lower river, and sometimes even some decent striped bass fishing add to the avid fisherman's list of options. Winchester Bay, at the mouth of the Umpqua, is the sport fishing capital of Oregon. Salmon Harbor, in the town of Winchester Bay, is the largest sport-boating basin on the coast, with more than 900 boat slips. The harbor provides easy access for private and charter boats to both the ocean and the river.

A three-mile drive to the east on Route 38 will take you to the Dean Creek Elk Viewing Area, managed by the Bureau of Land Management's Coos Bay District and the Oregon Department of Fish and Wildlife. Formerly a 900-acre ranch, the refuge is home year-round to a large herd of Roosevelt elk, the largest and perhaps most magnificent of the elk subspecies. The herd can be easily viewed and photographed at the site, and the stop is well worthwhile. Waterfowl, ospreys, bald eagles, and great blue herons might also be visible, so bring your binoculars. Two parking areas and an open-air interpretive center provide safe, informative viewing opportunities. There are also several pull-off/parking lanes along the three-mile stretch of Highway 38 that borders the area. Traffic along this highway is moderately heavy, however, so please exercise caution when entering or leaving these lanes

DUNES

One of the more dramatic and unusual landform features along the Oregon coast is the sand dune, which covers substantial areas of coastal terrain, especially near Sandlake and from Florence southward to Coos Bay. The dunes are spectacular, not to mention bleak, desolate, sterile, windy, harsh, photogenic, and awe-inspiring. The dunes are also dynamic; they continuously change in shape and form as they move across the landscape, paying little heed to the presence of trees, roads, or buildings. The cycle begins as sandstone in the Coast Range Mountains and near-shore terrain is eroded and carried to the sea by the numerous coastal rivers and streams. Ocean currents from the west then wash the sand up onto the beaches, where it dries and is blown inland by the prevailing winds.

The anatomy of a dune area typically includes a long, narrow foredune that parallels the beach. The sand here is usually stabilized by vegetation, especially grasses. Further inland is a zone called the deflation plain, a low-lying, wind-scoured area that is often eroded by the winds below the level of the local water table. The deflation plain therefore often contains small lakes, marshy areas, and lush vegetation, including such plants as willows, sedges, and even the tiny insectivorous (bug eating) sundew plant. Inland from the deflation plain may be found bands of sand ridges called transverse dunes, which are very actively moving and often contain quicksand. The large inland dunes are called oblique dunes because they lie at an oblique (slanted) angle to the shoreline. In some places they are over 500 feet high.

While at the dunes, look for tree-islands, remnants of earlier forests that have been isolated from the remaining forest by the movement of the dunes. These provide valuable wildlife habitat and are very sensitive to disturbance. In some places you can see forest graveyards, where the trees have been overtaken and killed by the moving sand. Only the tops of the dead trees sticking out above the sand surface provide evidence of the forests that formerly occupied these sites, creating an eerie feeling within the visitor to these forest skeletons.

The most spectacular dunes area is certainly the 47-mile stretch, 2 1/2 to 4 miles wide, that comprises the Oregon Dunes National Recreation Area (ODNRA). In addition to the dunes themselves, the ODNRA also includes 32 freshwater lakes, the mouths of the Umpqua and Siuslaw Rivers, and numerous marshes, estuaries, grasslands, and forests. About half of the area is open to off-road vehicle (ORV) use. Contact the ODNRA office in Reedsport for regulations. The best areas for hiking in the dunes are those that are off-limits to ORVs, and include the area between the Umpqua River estuary northward to Waxmyrtle Campground, and also the area just south of the Siuslaw River and just north of Tenmile Creek. Hikers should keep a careful eye on changing weather conditions and local landmarks. A sudden storm or fog can cut visibility to near zero, and the incessant winds can quickly remove footprints. In some places it may be difficult to retrace your path and find your way out of the dunes, especially if darkness is approaching. Be careful of dunebuggies coming over hilltops if you venture out into the ORV areas!

The dunes region is dotted with countless lakes on its eastern side, some very large and sprawling across the landscape like watery octopuses. These are prime fishing grounds for both warm and cold water species. Many bear Indian names, like Tahkenitch, Cleawox, and Woahink. These lakes were formed by the build-up of sand dunes that blocked stream flow to the ocean. They typically do not have stream outlets, but rather flow underground to the sea in a diffuse pattern through the porous sands.

and while viewing. If you have children, use the parking areas rather than the highway pull-offs.

South of Winchester Bay, Umpqua Lighthouse State Park provides excellent hiking in some of the largest coastal dunes (550 feet high) as well as great views and photographic opportunities, good birdwatching, and the 1894-vintage Umpqua River Light. The original lighthouse was completed in 1857, the first in the Oregon Territory. It was destroyed during the flood of 1861, and Congress did not appropriate funds for rebuilding until 1888. A quarter-mile hike along the Umpqua Dunes Trail from North Eel Campground will take you to an enormous expanse of sand containing some of the highest dunes. The trail around Lake Marie is beautiful. The nearby south jetty is very popular for fishing. A viewing platform near the Umpqua Lighthouse affords a good viewpoint for whale watching during migration. The grey whales occasionally come right into the mouth of the river. The platform includes panels of information on marine mammal ecology, and, like other coastal sites, is often manned by a whale-watching expert (volunteer) during the peak migrations.

Tenmile and North Tenmile Lakes are very popular for fishing, swimming, sailing, and waterskiing. These interconnected lakes are very large, with a multitude of coves and arms that provide pleasant exploration opportunities for canoeists. The lakes are shallow and contain good populations of a variety of warm-water and cold-water fish. These lakes may be among the best on the coast for catching bluegills with a five-year-old. The serious fisherman will also find some exciting prospects, particularly for largemouth bass. Boats and canoes can be rented at Lakeside Marina.

The adjacent communities of Coos Bay and North Bend constitute the largest metropolitan area on the Oregon coast. Activities center around the bay itself, the largest deep-water coastal port between San Francisco and Seattle. The local economy has been heavily dependent on logging and the wood products industry, and Coos Bay has been called the largest lumber-shipping port in the world. The bay and river provide a diversity of water-based recreation, including good fishing, crabbing, and clamming, as well as sailing, canoeing, and windsurfing. Salmon fishing can be very good in the bay, and in some years the bay provides a decent catch of striped bass. River Runner Harbor Cruises, located at the city dock, offers bay area cruises. Nearby Kentuck

Golf Course is the only 18-hole golf course on the south coast.

The Coos County Historical Museum, located in Simpson Park at the southern end of McCullough Bridge in North Bend, displays maritime artifacts and antique furniture. The Indian artifacts exhibits are excellent, especially the large collections of arrowheads and slingshots. Other interesting museums in the Coos Bay area include the Marshfield Sun Printing Museum, which displays the equipment of the historic printing operation (1891-1944), and the Coos Art Museum.

The Coos Bay area has a tremendous diversity of wintering birds (up to 150 species during Christmas bird counts), due to the large variety of habitat types found here. Jordan Cove is a great location for shorebirds at low tide. Pony Slough contains tremendous concentrations of wintering birds, and birding is generally best here at mid-tide. Shorebirds, waterfowl, great egrets, eared grebes, and short-eared owls are some of the species that top the list.

Charleston has a huge commercial fishing fleet and also excellent sport fishing opportunities. Local charter boats cross the bar in search of salmon and bottom fish. The best clamming is along the north spit, and crabbing can be quite good from the docks on the waterfront. The nearby University of Oregon's Institute of Marine Biology has an interpretive center, an outdoor aquarium, and hiking trails. The Coast Guard lookout is a great spot for photographers, offering excellent views of the bay and the fishing boats as they cross the bar.

The Cape Arago Highway extends south along some of the most scenic and picturesque coastline in the country. A series of enjoyable stops include Sunset Bay, Shore Acres, and Cape Arago State Parks. Sunset Bay is protected from the westerly winds and offers some relatively warm ocean water for swimming. Currents can be dangerous, however, and swimming should be only on incoming tides. This park also has some nice hiking trails, and the scenery is superb. A 3 1/2 mile trail follows the coast to just north of Cape Arago past the other two parks. Sunset Bay Golf Course is located adjacent to the state park. Designed by John Zoller, this course occupies 100 acres of scenic forest in the valley formed by Big Creek. The creek contributes to challenging play on eight of the nine holes, and is complemented by two small ponds.

Nearby Shore Acres is a magnificent garden spot on the former estate of Louis J. Simpson, a lumber and shipping magnate. Although the mansion burned down, the spectacular formal gardens have been preserved and restored, and are now maintained by the State. The park showcases thirty varieties of rhododendrons, as well as dozens of other kinds of trees and shrubs from around the world. Sunset Bay and Shore Acres State Parks both provide good birding, the former for marine birds and the latter for passerines. The rocky coastline throughout this area supports a good variety of shorebirds.

The third state park along this stretch is at Cape Arago, popular because of its views up and down the coast, good fishing from the rocky shoreline, and views of Simpson Reef, off-shore home to seals, sea lions and marine birds. The best vantage point for watching the marine mammals is from the turn-out just before the entrance to Cape Arago State Park. The cove just south of the point is accessible by a steep trail and contains some outstanding tidepools. The cove to the north is also excellent and contains an enormous intertidal area. Cape Arago Light Station is located a couple of miles north of the cape itself, and is a popular photographic subject, particularly from Lighthouse Beach. The lighthouse can also be photographed from the turn-out just north of the entrance to Shore Acres State Park.

All three state parks along the Cape Arago Highway offer year-round viewing of harbor seals, elephant seals, and sea lions. Whale watching is also good, including killer whales in early summer. Bird sightings may include peregrine falcons, brown pelicans, and bald eagles, as well as several species of marine birds on the rocks offshore.

The drive southward from the Coos Bay and Cape Arago area is pleasant and picturesque along the narrow and winding Seven Devils Road, which rejoins Highway 101 just north of Bandon. The road provides access to some excellent rock hounding spots at Whiskey Run and Agate Beaches. East of Cape Arago, off Seven Devils Road, is the South Slough National Estuarine Research Reserve. It contains 600 acres of tidal habitat and 3800 acres of upland forest, and supports a tremendous diversity of plants and animals. Canoeing and hiking are the activities of choice. Birdwatching and photographic opportunities are excellent. There is also an interpretive center and a busy program of summer activities, including guided walks, canoe tours, workshops, and children's programs. The main trail from the interpretive center will take you along coastal forests, salt marshes, a lookout with a panoramic view of the estuary, and rich coastal mudflats. For program information, call 888-5558, or write South Slough Reserve, P.O. Box 5417, Charleston, OR 97420.

BANDON TO THE CALIFORNIA BORDER

Often called Bandon-by-the-Sea, the charming coastal town of Bandon at the mouth of the Coquille River has much to offer the recreationist. The adjacent oceanfront is as photogenic as any along the coast, and is attractively dotted with numerous sea stacks that display a diversity of size and shape. Face Rock and Table Rock are two of the most noteworthy stacks. Face Rock received its name from its appearance and an ancient Indian legend. The daughter of Chief Siskiyou, a young maiden named Ewauna, is said to have perished in the sea, and her face is frozen in stone, smiling upwards at the clouds.

The historic Old Town, near the waterfront, has been recently renovated and is both attractive and interesting. Take an enjoyable stroll among the numerous galleries, shops and restaurants. The town was ravaged by fire twice since the turn of the century, most recently in 1936, and only about 16 of the original buildings remain. Activities include crabbing from the Bandon docks, charter fishing, and the popular stern wheeler rides up the Coquille River in the *Dixie Lee*. Also noteworthy is Bandon's cheddar cheese factory on the north end of town. On the southern end of town, near Face Rock, is a nine-hole public golf course. The nearby stables offer horseback riding and old-fashioned hay rides. Bandon has recently become a center for artists and craftsmen, and is the prime entertainment town on the south coast. The theater group, Encore Presenters, provides late-night entertainment, a rarity on the Oregon coast.

Just south of the jetty, the sea stacks provide nesting sites for marine birds, including a colony of 10,000 murres. Tufted puffins, pigeon guillemots, cormorants, and murrelets are also common. Wetlands to the north provide refuge to thousands of migrating birds. Bandon Marsh National Wildlife Refuge includes 289 acres of salt marsh at the mouth of the Coquille River. This area is especially important to migrating shorebirds and wintering water-

FISHING

The Oregon coast has so many outstanding fishing opportunities, it is difficult to know where to begin in describing the available options. There is a host of world-class salmon and steelhead waters that flow into the Pacific Ocean in Oregon. These are among the finest salmonid rivers in the United States south of Alaska. They include the Nestucca, Nehalem, Siuslaw, Alsea, Siletz, Wilson, Trask, Umpqua, Rogue, Elk, and Sixes Rivers. The salmon fishery also incudes open ocean fishing options, especially out of such ports as Brookings, Coos Bay, Depoe Bay, Newport, Garibaldi, Winchester Bay, Hammond, Warrenton, Astoria, and Florence.

With all of the excitement surrounding the salmon and steelhead fisheries, however, visitors often overlook many of the other fabulous fishing options available on the coast. Bottom-fishing charter services provide lots of off-shore action; surf-fishing and jetty-fishing are also excellent in many places.

South of Florence, the large dunes lakes provide some of the best bass fishing in Oregon, as well as great recreational fishing for the whole family. Siltcoos Lake and Tahkenitch Lake are outstanding. Tenmile and North Tenmile Lakes will yield all the bluegills your kindergartner can reel in. Lakes and streams with good to excellent trout fishing are scattered along the entire coast. To add some additional diversity, you may also want to try your luck for sturgeon in the Columbia River or striped bass in the south fork of the Coos River.

Besides the more traditional fishing activities with rod and reel, coastal visitors may wish to try clamming or crabbing as well. Clams can be dug at minus tides in most of the coastal bays and estuaries. The quarry include softshell clams, gapers, butter clams, littlenecks, and cockles. On some of the open-ocean beaches, digging for razor clams is very good. You only need boots, a shovel or rake (depending on species), a copy of this book, and a low tide in order to bring home a nice bucket of clams. It also doesn't hurt to know something about the species you are after, or carefully watch one of the "locals" and try to dig similarly. The razor clams are highly mobile, and you must dig quickly or they will escape. The bay clams, on the other hand, will stay put and retract their necks. The strategy here is to dig down a foot or two in close proximity to the clam hole. You then gradually cave the mud down, following the clam hole down until you reach the clam.

Crabbing is popular from the public docks available in many of the bays, but tends to be more successful from small boats out in the bays. Crabs are usually caught in a crab ring, which is baited with fish scraps and allowed to rest on the floor of the bay. Periodic retrieval of the ring will allow removal of the captured crabs. Check fishing regulations; you must throw back all females and small males.

---

fowl because so little salt marsh remains along the Pacific coast. Canoeing is also popular here. Much of the southern Oregon coast provides excellent birding during fall and winter. Regional highlights include, in addition to the mouth of the Coquille River, Cape Blanco, Humbug Mountain State Park, Boardman State Park, and the mouth of the Rogue River.

Salmon and steelhead fishing are good in both Coquille River and the bay. The docks provide good perch fishing. The commercial fishing fleet lands good quantities of salmon, tuna, halibut, and snapper. The lower river provides excellent crabbing.

Bandon is the cranberry capital of Oregon. The bogs are located both to the north and south of town. A September visit to coincide with the Cranberry Festival can be fun. Stop by the Bigwheel General Store to see part of Bill Magner's driftwood collection, "Abandoned-By-The-Sea-In-Bandon-By-The-Sea". This fascinating collection is reputed to be the largest driftwood collection in the world.

Across the Coquille River from Bandon is Bullards Beach State Park, a beautiful collection of beach, extensive dunes, and forest. It is a prime location for beachcombing and kite flying. There is a boat launch on the river, and the horse camp provides easy access for riding in the dunes and along the long stretch of beach. Strong winds also make the beach here an excellent source of driftwood. Herons and various species of shore birds are common in the adjacent mudflats along the river, whereas turnstones and oyster catchers are often seen among the rocks at the jetty. The Coquille River Light, built in 1896, has been preserved as an historical landmark and is the frequent subject of photographers' attention. Although located in the state park, it can also be nicely photographed from across the bay at the south jetty.

South of Bandon on Highway 101 is found the West Coast Game Park, where visitors can mingle with over 450 exotic animals of over 75 species, many of which can be petted. These include bison, lion, cougar, wolf, and llama. Children especially will find this an exciting stop. Further south at Langlois are found a Sports Museum and stables for horseback riding. Floras Lake is shallow and warm. Although just a short walk from the pounding surf of the Pacific Ocean, the lake enjoys consistent, and reasonably light, winds. It is a perfect place to learn the sport of windsurfing. Contact the Floras Lake Windsurfing School (telephone 347-9205) for details.

Hikers must exercise extreme caution along the southern Oregon coast. High tides totally cover most of the beaches, right up to the vertical cliffs. Pay particular attention to tides and weather conditions.

The hike along the beach from Bandon to Fourmile Creek is exceptional. Wide beaches parallel deserted sand dunes, lakes, and marshes on the east, and rugged coastline dotted with sea stacks on the west. If you continue south past Fourmile Creek, the hike takes you along a lengthy sandy spit between the ocean and New River. These beaches are among the most remote and inaccessible in Oregon.

The eight-mile long New River estuary was designated as an Area of Critical Environmental Concern (ACEC) by the BLM in 1983. The New River landscape is relatively undisturbed, and supports a wide array of rare plants and animals. In addition, outstanding recreational opportunities are present, including birding, canoeing, hiking, beach combing, hunting, and fishing.

The BLM's plans for New River include the purchase of all available lands bordering the river, control of grazing and off-road vehicle use, removal or control of the introduced European beach grass and Scotch broom, restoration of riparian habitat,

interpretation of prehistoric and historic cultural sites, development of day-use facilities and handicapped fishing access, and establishment of a field station to conduct coastal research and education.

Cape Blanco extends further west than any other point in the contiguous United States, and the off-shore environment can be quite hostile. The large grassy headland is crowned with the photogenic Cape Blanco Light. The lighthouse is perched high on the headland, 345 feet above the sea. It has been in operation since 1870, and is the oldest operating lighthouse in Oregon. Cape Blanco State Park has trails down the steep hillside to beaches that are popular for surf fishing and beachcombing. Whale watching is very good here. The extensive trail system on the cape makes this an attractive area for horseback riding, and a horse camp is available in the park. The Hughes House, an 1898 Victorian home, is open to the public in summer and contains a museum depicting historical photographs and displays of local ranching history. On either side of the cape, the Elk River and the Sixes River provide very good salmon, steelhead, and sea-run cutthroat fishing. Try your luck panning for gold in the river gravels.

Port Orford, attractively situated above a natural harbor sheltered by a small headland, is a small timber and commercial fishing community. It contains the best natural harbor between San Francisco and Puget Sound. The waterfront is atypical, in that a hoist system is used to dock vessels on top of a large wharf. There are no usual docks or moorage slips. It is the main Oregon port involved in the sea urchin fishery. Just north of town, Paradise Point Wayside provides access to a beautiful stretch of beach for hiking, agate collecting, and beachcombing. Battle Rock Wayside on the southern edge of town provides access to a nice beach and superb views from the rock south towards Humbug Mountain. Nearby Garrison Lake is popular for swimming, trout fishing, and waterskiing. It is also a great spot for windsurfing due to its close proximity to the coastline and constant winds.

The coastal drive from Port Orford to cone-shaped Humbug Mountain is quite pleasant. At 1756 feet, the mountain is the second highest on the coast and affords very good views. This is a good place for whale watching with a spotting scope or binoculars. Because the imposing mountain abuts the coastline, the highway skirts inland around it, providing a quick glimpse of the lush inland vegetation. Humbug Mountain State Park offers excellent hiking, particularly along a three-mile trail to the top of the mountain. There are two very good tidepool areas. The first is at Rocky Point on the northern edge of Humbug Mountain State Park. Hike 100 yards to the beach from a dirt road with limited parking. The second area can be reached via a 300-yard trail from the park's campground.

Prehistoric Gardens, south of Port Orford, is an unusual tourist attraction that contains scale models of dinosaurs and other prehistoric organisms in a rainforest setting. Pathways wind through the gardens and provide views of the animal replicas in life-like poses.

Gold Beach is a major tourist town on the south coast, largely because it happens to be situated on the south bank of the spectacular Rogue River. The Rogue is, without doubt, one of the finest rivers in the Pacific Northwest. The lower 50 miles or so are extremely popular for salmon and steelhead fishing, jet boat rides, and general sightseeing. The upper stretch, designated as a Wild and Scenic River, is prime country for white-water rafting and kayaking. Permits are required during the popular summer months in the Wild and Scenic section, although access is available anytime on the lower section and also inland near Grants Pass. Upriver can be found a string of wilderness lodges along the Rogue River Trail. They are spaced a comfortable distance apart for leisurely backpacking without carrying a lot of gear. Contact the lodge owners to make arrangements:

Illahe Lodge	247-6111
Wild River Lodge	826-9453
Clay Hill Lodge	826-9453
Paradise Bar Lodge	247-6022
Half Moon Bar	476-4002
Marial Lodge	474-2057

Gold was discovered in the Rogue River basin in 1852. Several years of not-very-productive placer mining of the beach sands ended when a flood washed most of the sand, and its precious cargo, out to sea. In more recent years, local attention has shifted from gold to fishing and tourism. A local group, known as the Rogue Pacific Interpretive Center, offers a variety of natural resource educational and recreational opportunities in Gold Beach. Workshops include whale-watching, coastal geology, tidepooling, clamming, and children's nature crafts.

Hydro-jet mail boats provide scenic excursions up the Rogue River from Gold Beach. Several trip options are available, including the mail run upriver to Agnes, which has been on-going for the past 90 years. This six-hour, 64-mile cruise through the canyons of the lower Rogue offers spectacular scenery and wildlife viewing. Bald eagles, deer, beaver, and many other species are common. Eighty- and 104-mile excursions into rugged whitewater sections of the river are also available, and provide excitement as well as scenery.

The Rogue River was made famous as a fishing river by author Zane Gray, who loved to fish the Rogue and frequently wrote about it. The lower river provides exceptional chinook salmon and steelhead fishing. Gold Beach is also a popular port for ocean fishing, mainly salmon and bottom fish, although the very difficult Rogue River bar often limits access to the ocean for sport fishing boats. Seals and sea lions are frequently seen in the lower river and along the jetty. Ospreys and a wide variety of species of ducks are very common. River otters are also present in the river a mile upstream from Gold Beach.

The coastline between Gold Beach and Brookings is among the most scenic stretches of the entire coast. Numerous headlands and points, rugged bluffs and mountains, small coves and beaches, and hundreds of islands and sea stacks are interspersed in a pattern of incredible diversity and beauty. The major headlands include Cape Sebastian, Crook Point, Sand Hill, and Cape Ferrelo. Cape Sebastian State Park, Pistol River State Park, and Samuel Boardman State Park occupy the majority of this 28-mile coastal strip. At Cape Sebastian, a short hike provides exceptional views, and the trail continues a couple of miles down to the shore. This park is known for its wildflower display in late April and May. Pacific paintbrush, Douglas iris, snow-queen, and gold-fields highlight the colorful floral diversity of the cape. The beach north of Meyer's Creek offers excellent tidepooling around the numerous near-shore sea stacks, and also great clamming for razor clams.

Boardman State Park is spectacular. Huge bluffs and steep cliffs plunge directly into the sea along about 10 miles of coastline. Small coves and beaches, numerous off-shore sea stacks and arches, huge canyons carved by coastal streams, and magnificent forests create some of the most impressive coastal scenery imaginable. There are 10 or more dramatic waysides and viewpoints along this stretch of coastline. The highway crosses 345 feet above a small stream at Thomas Creek Bridge, the highest coastal bridge north of San Francisco. Some particularly worthwhile stopping places include Arch Rock, Natural Bridges Cove, Bruces Bones Creek, Indian Sands Beach, Whale-Head Cove, Houserock Viewpoint on Cape Ferrelo, the tip of Cape Ferrelo, and Lone Ranch Beach. Activities at any and all of these stops are basically the same: hike the short trails, dig razor clams on the beaches, fish off the rocks and in the surf, look for whales, lay on the beach in the sun, take lots of pictures, and wonder at the rugged beauty of the best Oregon has to offer.

It is only fitting that this stretch of coastline is named after Samuel Boardman. From 1929 to 1950, as Superintendent of Oregon's Parks, he supervised the acquisition of over 50,000 acres of spectacular parks for the state, much of which by donation, and developed the best state parks system in the United States. His foresight and creative energy were largely responsible for preserving the unspoiled beauty of the Oregon coast. Oregonians and visitors will be forever indebted to Mr. Boardman.

Between Boardman State Park and Brookings lies a region of geographical diversity and dramatic relief. The Coast Range Mountains crowd in steeply along the coastline, and there are alternating areas of sandy beach, rocky points, and magnificent sea stacks. Harris Beach State Park is beautiful. It contains several good tidepool areas; the main one is directly west of the campground. Twenty-one acre Goat Island is the largest of the offshore islands in the state and is home to a multitude of sea birds.

The coastal town of Brookings is situated on the north bank of the Chetco River. The community depends heavily on logging, wood products, agriculture, and commercial fishing. Easter lilies are grown here in abundance, due largely to unusual meteorological conditions that keep winter temperatures warmer in Brookings than anywhere else in the state. About 90% of all the Easter lilies sold in the United States are grown here, in Oregon's "banana belt". The historical museum, south of the harbor, is an interesting stop. Adjacent to the museum is found the largest cyprus tree in the world. It has a girth of over 30 feet.

The Chetco River flows out of the Kalmiopsis Wilderness in the Siskiyou Mountains to the east, and is known for its hiking and backpacking opportunities. Designated as a wild and scenic river, the Chetco has excellent fishing for coho and chinook salmon and steelhead. Twenty-pound steelhead, and chinook more than twice that size, are not uncommon. Because of its protected southerly orientation, and safe bar, Chetco Bay is the top port on the Oregon Coast for off-shore small-craft salmon fishing. The average annual catch of fall salmon is about 25,000 fish, split about equally between coho and chinook.

Eight miles up the Chetco River, in Loeb State Park, can be found Oregon's largest stand of old-growth myrtlewood trees. The wood of the myrtlewood is highly prized for its grain and coloration, and is very popular for making Oregon gift items: bowls, plates, and decorative objects.

We hope you have enjoyed your tour of the Oregon coast. With the help of this book, perhaps you will plan additional trips to what we believe to be the finest stretch of coastline in the United States. Please write and share your coastal experiences with us. We would love to hear from you.

SOURCES OF INFORMATION

State of Oregon

Oregon State Parks and Recreation	525 Trade St. SE, Salem, OR 97310	378-6305
State Parks Campground Information Center		238-7488 1-800-452-5687 (Oregon)
State Parks and Recreation Regional Offices Tillamook Coos Bay	3600 E. Third Street 365 N. 4th St., Suite A	842-5501 269-9410
Oregon Department of Fish and Wildlife	P.O. Box 59, Portland, OR 97207	229-5403
Oregon Department of Geology	1400 SW 5th St., Portland, OR 97201	229-5580
Oregon Marine Board	3000 Market Street NE, Salem, OR 97310	378-8587
Oregon Department of Transportation	325 13th St. NE, Salem, OR 97310	373-7356
Oregon Economic Development Dept., Tourism Division	595 College St., NE, Salem, OR 97310	378-3451 1-800-233-3306 (Oregon)
Oregon Department of Forestry	2600 State St., Salem, OR 97310	378-2560

Federal Government

U.S. Bureau of Land Management (BLM)	P.O. Box 2965, Portland, OR 97208	231-6274
BLM Regional Office	1300 Airport Lane, North Bend, OR 97459	756-0100
U.S. Fish and Wildlife Service	1002 NE Holladay St., Portland, OR 97232	231-6828
U.S. Forest Service	P.O. Box 3623, Portland, OR 97208	326-2877
Oregon Dunes Natl. Recreation Area	Siuslaw N.F., 855 Hyway Ave., Reedsport, OR 97467	271-3611
Siuslaw National Forest, Waldport Ranger District	Waldport, OR	563-3211
South Slough Natl. Estuarine Reserve	P.O. Box 5417, Charleston, OR 97420	888-5558
Cape Perpetua Visitors Center	P.O. Box 274, Yachats, OR 97498	
U.S. Forest Service, Chetco Ranger Station	555 Fifth Street, Brookings, OR	469-2196
U.S. Forest Service, Gold Beach Ranger Station	1225 S. Ellensburg, Gold Beach, OR	247-6651

Chambers of Commerce and Visitor Centers

Astoria Area Chamber of Commerce	P.O. Box 176, Astoria, OR 97103	325-6311
Seaside Chamber of Commerce	P.O. Box 7, Seaside, OR 97138	738-6391 1-800-444-6740
Cannon Beach Chamber of Commerce	P.O. Box 64, Cannon Beach, OR 97110	436-2623
Nehalem Bay Area Chamber of Commerce	P.O. Box 238, Wheeler, OR 97147	368-7153
Rockaway Beach Chamber of Commerce	P.O. Box 198, Rockaway Beach, OR 97136	355-8108
Garibaldi Chamber of Commerce	P.O. Box 5, Garibaldi, OR 97118	322-0301
Tillamook Chamber of Commerce	3705 Hwy 101 N, Tillamook, OR 97141	842-7525 842-7526
Pacific City-Woods Chamber of Commerce	P.O. Box 331, Pacific City, OR 97135	965-6161
Lincoln City Chamber of Commerce	P.O. Box 787, Lincoln City, OR 97367	994-3070 1-800-452-2151 (Oregon)
Depoe Bay Chamber of Commerce	P.O. Box 21, Depoe Bay, OR 97341	765-2889
Newport Chamber of Commerce	555 SW Coast Hwy, Newport, OR 97365	265-8801 1-800-262-7844
Waldport Chamber of Commerce	P.O. Box 669, Waldport, OR 97394	563-2133
Yachats Chamber of Commerce	P.O. Box 174, Yachats, OR 97498	547-3530
Florence Chamber of Commerce	P.O. Box 26000, Florence, OR 97439	997-3128
Reedsport-Lower Umpqua Chamber of Commerce	P.O. Box 11-B, Reedsport, OR 97467	271-3495 1-800-247-2155 (Oregon)
Lakeside Chamber of Commerce	P.O. Box 333, Lakeside, OR 97449	759-3001
North Bend Information Center	P.O. Box B, North Bend, OR 97459	756-4613
Bay Area Chamber of Commerce	P.O. Box 210, Coos Bay, OR 97420	269-0215 1-800-762-6278 (Oregon) 1-800-824-8486 (Out of State)
Charleston Information Center	P.O. Box 5735, Charleston, OR	888-2311
Coquille Chamber of Commerce	119 N. Birch St., Coquille, OR 97423	396-3414
Bandon-By-The Sea Chamber of Commerce	P.O. Box 1515, Bandon, OR 97411	347-9616
Myrtle Point Chamber of Commerce	424 5th Street, Myrtle Point, OR 97458	572-2626

Port Orford Chamber of Commerce	P.O. Box 637, Port Orford, OR 97465	332-8055
Gold Beach Chamber of Commerce	510 S. Ellensburg, Gold Beach, OR 97444	247-7526 1-800-452-2334 (Oregon) 1-800-542-2334 (Out of State)
Brookings-Harbor Chamber of Commerce	P.O. Box 940, Brookings, OR 97415	469-3181

Other

Oregon Guides and Packers Assoc.	P.O. Box 10841, Eugene, OR 97440	683-9552
Oregon Coast Association	P.O. Box 670, Newport, OR 97365	1-800-982-6278 585-9130
Hatfield Marine Science Center	South Beach, Newport	867-0100
Portland Audubon Society	5151 NW Cornell Rd., Portland, OR 97210	292-6855
Coastal Zone Management Association	P.O. Box 1033, Newport, OR 97365	265-8918
Oregon Coastline Express (railway)	4000 Hangar Rd., Tillamook, OR 97141	842-2768
Sea Lion Caves	91560 Highway 101, Florence, OR 97439	547-3111
The Nature Conservancy	1205 NW 25th Ave., Portland, OR 97210	228-9561
West Coast Game Park	Rt. 1, Box 1330, Bandon, OR 97411	347-3106
Recreational Opportunity Guide	855 Hwy Ave., Reedsport, OR 97467	271-3611
Rogue Pacific Interpretive Center	510 Colvin St., Gold Beach, OR 97444	247-2732
Floras Lake Windsurfing School	P.O. Box 1591, Bandon, OR 97411	347-9205

CAMPGROUNDS

Campground	Type	Campsites Tent	Trailer/RV	Total	Address	Phone
Astoria/Warrenton						
Fort Stevens	SP*	262	343	605	Hammond	861-1671
Kampers West		100	100	200	1140 NW Warrenton Dr.	861-1814
Sunset West					Warrenton	861-1760
Hammond						
KOA				83	1100 NW Ridge Road	861-2606
Seaside						
Bud's Campground		0	24	24	Hwy 101, 1 mi. N of Gearhart	738-6855
Riverside Lake Resort		30	39	69	W of Hwy 101, 1.5 mi. S of Seaside	738-6779
Venice Trailer Park		0	30	30	1032 24th Ave.	738-8851
Seaside RV					1445 S. Holladay Dr.	738-8664
Circle Creek RV & Campground					Highway 101	738-6070
Cannon Beach						
Oswald West	SP	36	0	36	10 mi. S of Cannon Beach (walk-in only)	368-5943
Cannon Beach RV		0	100	100	345 Elk Creek Rd., E of Hwy 101, Cannon Beach	436-2231
Sea Ranch Resort		33	38	71	N of Cannon Beach	436-2815
Nehalem						
Nehalem Bay	SP	0	291	291	3 mi. S of Manzanita Jct.	368-5154
Nehalem Shores RV		0	25	25	1 mi. N of Nehalem	368-6670
Rockaway Beach						
Jetty Fishery		15	15	30	27550 Hwy 101 N, 3 mi. N of Rockaway Beach	368-5746
Shorewood Travel Trailer Park		0	105	105	W of Hwy 101, 1 mi. S of Rockaway Beach	355-2278
Spring Lake RV Park					8015 Pansy St., Rockaway Beach	355-2411
Garibaldi						
Barview Jetty County Pk.	CP	190	60	250	Barview, NW of Garibaldi	322-3522
Kilchis County Park	CP				8 mi. N of Tillamook	

Campground	Type	Campsites			Address	Phone
		Tent	Trailer/RV	Total		
Tillamook						
Cape Lookout	SP*	197	53	250	13000 Whiskey Creek Rd. W., 12 mi. SW of Tillamook	842-4981
Pacific Campground		0	75	75	2 mi. N of Tillamook	842-5201
Tillamook KOA		2	83	85	6 mi. S of Tillamook	842-4779
Netarts						
Bay Shore Trailer Park		0	58	58	Three Capes Loop, Netarts	842-7774
Happy Camp Resort		0	71	71	Netarts	842-4012
Big Spruce Trailer Park		0	23	23	Netarts	842-7443
Happy Camp		0	36	36	Netarts	842-4012
Pacific City						
Cape Kiwanda RV	FS	0	130	130	Pacific City	965-6230
Sandlake Campground	FS			215	7000 Galloway Rd., Cloverdale, W of Three Capes Loop at Sandlake Grocery	965-6097
Sand Beach	FS			101	9 mi. N of Pacific City	
Whalen Island	CP				5 mi. N of Pacific City	
Raines Resort		2	12	14	NW of Pacific City	965-6371
Webb Park	CP			30	2 mi. N of Pacific City	
Wood Park	CP	5	5	10	1 mi. N of Pacific City	
Neskowin						
Neskowin Creek RV		0	49	49	50500 Hwy 101 South	392-3120
Lincoln City						
Devil's Lake	SP*	68	32	100	1452 NE 6th, Lincoln City	994-2002
KOA Campground		42	38	80	East Devil's Lake Rd., N of Devil's Lake	994-2961
Coyote Rock RV		0	58	58	Hwy 229, SE of Lincoln City	996-3436
Sportsman's Landing		0	30	30	Hwy 229, SE of Lincoln City	996-4225
Depoe Bay						
Holiday RV		0	110	110	North side of Depoe Bay	765-2302
Fogarty Creek RV		0	53	53	2 mi. N of Depoe Bay	764-2228
Sea & Sand RV		9	86	95	3.5 mi. N of Depoe Bay	764-2313
Newport						
Beverly Beach	SP*	152	127	279	6.3 mi. N of Newport	265-9278

Name	Type				Location	Phone
South Beach	SP*	254	254	0	2 mi. S of Newport	867-4715
Newport Marina & RV		38	38	0	600 SE Bay Blvd., at South Beach, Newport	867-3321
Pacific Shores RV		287	287	0	3 mi. N of Newport	265-3750 / 1-800-666-6313
Whalers Rest		99	99	0	Hwy. 101 at South Beach	867-3100
Harbor Village RV		140	140	0	923 SE Bay Blvd.	265-5088
Sportsman's Trailer Pk.		40	40	0	Marine Science Dr., South Beach	867-9588
Surfside Mobile Vill.		8	8	0	392 NW 3rd	265-2109
Agate Beach RV		32	32	0	6138 N. Hwy 101	265-7670
City Center Trailer Pk.		55	55	0	721 N. Hwy. 101	265-5731
Waldport						
Seal Rock Trailer Court	SP*	44	44	0	Seal Rock	563-3955
Beachside		80	60	20	4 mi. S of Waldport	563-3220
Handy Haven RV		11	11	0	Waldport	563-4286
King Silver Trailer Park		26	26	0	3.6 mi. E of Waldport	563-3502
Fishin' Hole Park & Marina		21	21	0	3.8 mi. E of Waldport	563-3401
Chinook Trailer Park		15	15	0	3.3 mi. E of Waldport	563-3485
Drift Creek Landing		60	60	0	3.7 mi. E of Waldport	563-3610
Yachats						
Carl G. Washburne	SP	66	58	8	U.S. Hwy 101, 14 mi. S of Yachats	547-3416
Cape Perpetua Cmpgrnd.	FS	37			Cape Perpetua, 2.5 mi. S of Yachats	547-3289
Sea Perch Campground		48	48	0	95480 Hwy 101, 5.8 mi. S of Yachats	547-3505
Tillicum Beach Cmpgrnd.	FS	57			4.5 mi. S of Waldport	563-3211
Rock Creek	FS	16	0	16	10 mi. S of Yachats	
Florence						
Jessie M. Honeyman	SP*	381	141	240	84505 Hwy 101, 3 mi. S of Florence	997-3641
Carter Lake Campground	FS	22			W of Hwy 101, 11 mi. S of Florence	271-3611
Alder Lake Campground	FS	20	20	0	N of Florence	
Dune Lake Campground	FS	17	17	0	N of Florence	
Driftwood II ORV Campground	FS	70	70	0	W of Hwy 101 on Siltcoos Beach Access Rd., 10 mi. S of Florence	271-3611
Lagoon Campground	FS	40			W of Hwy 101 on Siltcoos Beach Access Rd., 10 mi. S of Florence	
Siuslaw Harbor Vista	CP	26			4 mi. NW of Florence, Rhododendron Dr.	271-3611
Sutton Lake	CP				5 mi. N of Florence	
Sutton Creek	FS	91			N of Florence	

Campground	Type	Campsites			Address	Phone
		Tent	Trailer/RV	Total		
Tyee Campground	FS	14	0	14	Westlake Rd., E of Hwy 101, 6 mi. S of Florence	271-3611
Waxmyrtle Campground	FS		56	56	Siltcoos Beach Access Rd., W of Hwy 101, 10 mi., S of Florence	271-3611
Carter Lake East	FS	0	11	11		
Florence Dunes KOA		32	94	126	Rhododendron Drive	997-6431
Port of Siuslaw RV		0	78	78	Florence	997-3040
Siltcoos Lake Resort		0	12	12	6 mi. S of Florence	997-3741
Darling's Resort & Trailer Park			15		4879 Darling's Loop, Florence	997-2841
Woahink Lake Resort RV					83570 Hwy 101, S. of Florence	997-6454
Reedsport/Winchester Bay						
Umpqua Lighthouse	SP	42	22	64	6 mi. S of Reedsport	271-4118
Surfwood Campground		22	141	163	2.5 mi. S of Reedsport	271-4020
Tahkenitch Campground	FS	0		36	7 mi. N of Reedsport	271-3611
Tahkenitch Landing	FS	0	26	26	7 mi. N of Reedsport	271-3611
Windy Cove County Park		0	75	75	3 mi. S of Reedsport	271-4138
Coho Marina & RV	CP	0	49	49	Reedsport	271-4676
Lakeside						
William M. Tugman	SP	0	115	115	U.S. Hwy 101, 8 mi. S of Reedsport	271-3611
Mid Eel Creek Cmpgrnd.	FS			25	ODNRA, W of Hwy 101 at Lakeside Junction	271-3611
North Eel Creek Cmpgrnd	FS			53	ODNRA, W of Hwy 101 at Lakeside Junction	
North Lake Resort & Marina		64	36	100	2090 North Lake Rd., on SW end of North Lake	759-3515
Coos Bay						
Bluebill Campground	FS	0	19	19	ODNRA, on Bluebill Lake, 2.8 mi. W of Hwy 101, Jordan Cove Rd.	
Horsfall Staging Area Campground	FS	0	70	70	ODNRA, 1.7 mi. W of Hwy 101, Jordan Cove Rd.	
Lucky Logger RV		0	78	78	250 E. Johnson, Coos Bay	267-6003
The Firs Trailer Park		0	25	25	N of N. Bend	756-6274
Charleston						
Sunset Bay	SP*	109	29	138	13030 Cape Arago Hwy, 3.6 mi. S of Charleston	888-4902
Basterdorf Beach County Park	CP	25	56	81	2 mi. SW of Charleston	888-5353

Campground	Type				Location	Phone
Seaport RV		0	26	26	Boat Basin Drive, off Cape Arago Hwy	888-3122
Charleston Marina & Travel Park		12	88	100	Kingfisher Dr., off Boat Basin Dr.	888-9512
Driftwood RV		0	15	15	Highway 240, N. of Charleston	888-6103
Kelly's RV		0	38	38	Highway 240, N. of Charleston	888-6531
Plainview Trailer Park		0	34	34	Highway 240, N. of Charleston	888-5166
Bandon						
Bullard's Beach	SP	0	192	192	U.S. Hwy 101, 2 mi. N of Bandon	347-3501
Blue Jay		20	20	40	S of Bandon on Beach Loop	347-3258
Driftwood Shores RV		0	40	40	Bandon	347-4122
Pine Springs KOA					Hwy 101, Langlois	348-2358
Port Orford						
Cape Blanco	SP	0	58	58	9 mi. NW of Port Orford	332-6774
Humbug Mountain	SP	78	30	108	U.S. Hwy 101, 6 mi. S of Port Orford	332-5942
Evergreen RV		0	11	11	839 Coast Guard Rd.	
Arizona Beach Resort		31	96	127	36939 Hwy. 101	332-6491
Gold Beach						
Four Seasons RV		0	45	45	96526 N. Bank Rogue Rd., 6 1/2 mi. E of Hwy 101	247-7959
Indian Creek Rec. Park		25	100	125	South bank of Rogue R., 1/2 mi. E of Hwy 101	247-7704
Honey Bear Campground		86	64	150	Old Hwy 101 at Ophir, P.O. Box 97, Ophir, OR	247-2765
Secret Camp RV		0	20	20	95614 Jerry's Flat Rd.	247-2665
Oceanside RV					S. Jetty Road	247-2301
Nesika Beach RV		10	27	37	Nesika Rd., Nesika	247-6077
Angler's Trailer Village		0	40	40	95706 Jerry's Flat Rd.	247-7922
Kimball Crk. Bend Resort		10	56	66	97136 N. Bank Rogue Rd.	247-7580
Sandy Camp/RV		50	36	86	South Jetty Rd.	247-2301
Brookings						
River Bend Park	SP*	0	120	120	Southbank Chetco River Rd.	469-3356
Harris Beach		66	85	151	1665 Hwy 101, Brookings	469-2021
Beachfront RV		0	173	173	16024 Boat Basin Dr.	469-5867
Chetco RV		0	121	121	16117 Hwy 101 South	469-3863
Driftwood RV		0	100	100	16011 Lower Harbor Rd.	469-3213
Whaleshead RV					N of Brookings	
Port of Brookings		0	173	173	Benham Lane, Brookings	469-5867

SP = state park; * indicates reservations accepted; 1-800-452-5687 in OR, (503) 238-7488 out of Oregon, for information on availability.

CP = county park; FS = Forest Service campground

GOLF COURSES

Course	Location	Type	Holes	Phone
Astoria Golf & Country Club	SE of Warrenton	Private	18	861-2545
Gearhart Golf Links	N. Marion, Gearhart	Public	18	738-5248
Highlands Golf Course	1.3 mi N of Gearhart	Public	9	738-0959
Seaside Golf Club	451 Avenue U, Seaside	Public	9	738-5261
Manzanita Golf Course	Lakeview Drive, Manzanita	Public	9	368-5744
Alderbrook Golf Club	7300 Alderbrook Rd., NE of Tillamook	Public	18	842-6413
Neskowin Beach Golf Course	1 Hawk Ave., Neskowin	Public	9	392-3377
Hawk Creek Golf Club	48480 S Hwy 101, Neskowin	Public	9	392-4120
Devil's Lake Golf & Racket	3245 Club House Dr., N. of Lincoln City	Public	13	994-8442
Salishan Golf Links	Gleneden Beach	Public	18	764-3632
Agate Beach Golf Club	4100 NE Golf Course Dr. N. of Newport	Public	9	265-7331
Ollala Valley Golf Course	1022 Olalla Rd., Toledo	Public	9	336-2121
Crestview Hills Golf Course	1680 Crestline Dr. S. of Waldport	Public	9	563-9020
Ocean Dunes Golf Links	3315 Munsel Lake Rd., N. of Florence	Public	9	997-3232
Forest Hills Golf Course	1 Country Club Dr., Reedsport	Semi-Private	9	271-2626
Kentuck Golf Course	E. Bay Dr., North Bend	Public	18	756-4464
Sunset Bay Golf Course	11001 Cape Arago Hwy, by Sunset Bay Campground, near Charleston	Public	9	888-9301
Coquille Valley Elks Club	Myrtle Point	Private	9	572-5367
Coos Country Club	999 Sumner Rd., Coos Bay	Semi-Private	9	267-7257
Bandon Face Rock Golf Course	3235 Beach Loop Rd.	Public	9	347-3818
Cedar Bend Golf Course	Squaw Valley Rd., 11 mi N of Gold Beach	Public	9	247-6911

HORSEBACK RIDING

Stables

Faraway Farms	P.O. Box 290, Seaside, OR 97138	738-6336
Sea Ranch RV Park	415 N. Hemlock, P.O. Box 214 Cannon Beach, OR 97110	436-2815
C&M Stables	90241 N. Hwy 101, Florence, OR 97439	997-7540
Bandon Stables	2747 Beach Loop Drive, Bandon, OR 97411	347-9181
Stone Butte Stables	46509 Hwy 101, Langois, OR	348-2525
Indian Creek Trail Rides	Jerry's Flat Road, 1/2 mi. E of Gold Beach	247-7704

Horse Hotels

Broken Bone Ranch	P.O. Box 39, Neotsu, OR 97364	994-8811
Family Four Stables	255 Transit Hill, North Bend, OR 97459	756-7466 or 267-5859

Horse Camps

Wildmare Horse Campground	Ore. Dunes National Rec. Area 855 Highway Ave., Reedsport, OR 97467	271-3611
Nehalem Bay State Park	8300 3rd Street Necarney, Nahalem Bay, OR 97131	368-5943 (Park) 842-5501 (Regional Off.)
Bullards Beach State Park Horse Camp	P.O. Box 25, Bandon, OR 97411	347-2209
Cape Blanco State Park	North of Port Orford	332-6774

MARINA AND MOORAGE FACILITIES

Name	Water Body	Location	Facilities			
			ramp	moorage	fuel	marine supplies
Hammond Mooring Basin	Columbia River	Mouth of Columbia, at Hwy 104	+	+		
Warrenton Marina	Skipanon River	.25 mi E of business dist. in Warrenton	+	+		+
West Mooring Basin	Columbia River	Hwy 30, Basin Ave. at Red Lion Hotel		+		
Youngs Bay Landing	Youngs Bay	3 mi E of Astoria on Hwy 202	+	+	+	+
Nehalem Shores	Nehalem River	1 mi NE of Nehalem		+	+	+
Nehalem Bay Ramp	Nehalem Bay	.5 mi S of Nehalem on Hwy 101	+	+		
Nehalem Park	Nehalem Bay	In Nehalem on Hwy 101		+		
Wheeler Marina	Nehalem Bay	Wheeler Waterfront on Hwy 101		+	+	+
Paradise Cove Resort	Nehalem Bay	S of Wheeler on Hwy 101	+		+	+
Brighton Moorage	Nehalem Bay	5 mi N of Rockaway on Hwy 101	+		+	+
Jetty Fishery	Nehalem Bay	3 mi N of Rockaway Beach, Hwy 101	+		+	+
Garibaldi Marina	Tillamook Bay	1/8 mi W of Garibaldi	+		+	+
Port of Bay City	Tillamook Bay	Boat Basin in Garibaldi	+		+	+
Big Barn Marina & RV Park	Tillamook River	1 mi NE of Tillamook on Hwy 131	+	+	+	+
Netarts Landing & Marina	Netarts Bay	In Netarts at N end of bay	+	+		
Nestucca Country Sptg. Gds	Nestucca River	2 mi off Hwy 101 on Pacific City Loop	+	+	+	+
Siletz Moorage	Siletz River	Jct of Siletz Hwy & Hwy 101 bridge	+	+	+	+
Coyote Rock RV Park	Siletz River	3 mi S of Lincoln City on Hwy 229	+	+	+	+
Sportsmans Landing	Siletz River	4 mi E of Hwy 101 on Hwy 229	+		+	
City of Depoe Bay	Depoe Bay	S side of bridge in Depoe Bay	+	+		+
Newport Marina	Yaquina Bay	1 mi E of Hwy 101	+	+		
Embarcadero Dock	Yaquina Bay	1 mi E of Hwy 101 in Newport	+	+	+	+
South Beach Marina	Yaquina Bay	Near Marine Science Center	+	+	+	+
Idaho Point Marina	Yaquina Bay	1 mi E of Hwy 101	+	+		
River Bend Moorage	Yaquina Bay	5 mi E on Bay Rd from downtown	+	+	+	+
Sawyers Moorage	Yaquina Bay	4 mi E on Bay Rd	+	+	+	+
Port of Alsea	Alsea Bay	5 blks off Hwy 101 in Waldport	+		+	+
McKinley's Marina	Alsea Bay	1 mi E of Waldport on Hwy 34	+		+	+
King Silver	Alsea River	E of Waldport	+	+	+	
Drift Creek Landing	Alsea River	3.7 mi E of Hwy 101 on Hwy 34	+	+	+	+
Fishin' Hole Trailer Park	Alsea River	4 mi E of Waldport off Hwy 34	+		+	+
Oaklands Marina	Alsea River	4.2 mi E of Waldport	+		+	+
Happy Landing	Alsea River	Hwy 34 Crossing at MP7, E of Waldport	+	+	+	
Taylors Landing	Alsea River	7.1 mi E of Waldport on Hwy 34	+	+		+

Name	Water Body	Location	Facilities			
			ramp	moorage	fuel	marine supplies
Kozy Kove	Alsea River	Tidewater at MP 9.5, E of Waldport	+	+	+	+
Tahkenitch Fishing Village	Tahkenitch Lake	NW of Reedsport on Hwy 101 at bridge		+	+	
Salmon Harbor	Winchester Bay	.25 mi W of Hwy 101, Salmon Hrbr. Blvd.	+	+	+	+
Gardiner	Umpqua River	On Hwy 101 in Gardiner	+		+	+
Lakeside Marina	Tenmile Lake	1 mi E of Hwy 101, end of 8th St.		+	+	+
North Lake Resort & Marina	Tenmile Lake	In Lakeside, 1500 Blk of N. Lake Rd.	+	+	+	+
Loon Lake Lodge Resorts	Loon Lake	9 mi S of Hwy 38, near Scottsburg	+		+	
Charleston Boat Basin	Coos Bay	Charleston	+		+	+
Mercer Lake Resort	Mercer Lake	5 mi N of Florence, E off Hwy 101	+	+	+	
Cushman RV & Marina	Siuslaw River	3 mi E of Hwy 101 at RR Bridge	+	+	+	+
Siuslaw Marina	Siuslaw River	3 mi E of Florence on Hwy 126	+	+	+	+
Florence Public Ramp	Siuslaw River	Florence waterfront	+	+	+	+
Bay Bridge Marina	Siuslaw River	1/8 mi off Hwy 101 in Florence			+	
Westlake Resort	Siltcoos Lake	6 mi S of Florence, Westlake exit	+		+	
Siltcoos Lake Resort	Siltcoos Lake	2 blks off Hwy 101 at Westlake Jct.	+		+	
Fishmill Lodges	Siltcoos Lake	Off Hwy 101 to W shore of Siltcoos Lk	+		+	+
Ada Resort	Siltcoos Lake	13 mi SE of Honeyman SP	+			+
Nightengale's Resort	Siltcoos Lake	Across from Honeyman SP, follow signs	+	+	+	
Midway Dock	Siuslaw River	5 mi E of Florence on Hwy 126	+		+	
C&D Dock	Siuslaw River	8 mi E of Florence on Hwy 126	+		+	
Port of Bandon	Coquille River	In Bandon	+	+		+
Port of Port Orford	Pacific Ocean	2 blks off Hwy 101 in Port Orford	+		+	
Jot's Resort	Rogue River Bay	N of Gold Beach on Hwy 101	+	+	+	+
Port of Gold Beach	Rogue River Bay	In Gold Beach	+		+	+
Port of Brookings Harbor	Chetco River	.5 mi S of Brookings	+	+	+	+

ANNUAL EVENTS

Astoria
Greater Astoria Crab Feed and Seafood Festival - April
Scandinavian Midsummer Festival - June
Astoria Regatta - maritime celebration, parade, food and craft booths, beer garden - August
Great Columbia Crossing - 8 1/2 mile run across the Astoria Bridge - October
Clatsop County Fair - August
Oregon Dixieland Jubilee - October
Santa Lucia Festival of Lights - November
Fort Clatsop National Memorial Holiday Program - December

Seaside
Trail's End Marathon - February
Beachcomber Festival - February
Miss Oregon Pageant - July
Dahlia Festival - August
Volleyball Tournament on the Beach - August
Seaside Beach Run - August
Cruisin' the Turnaround - September
Oktoberfest - September
Great Pumpkin Party - October
Christmas Gift Fair - November

Cannon Beach
Kite Festival - April
Sandcastle Day - June
Children's Parade - June
Stormy Weather Festival - November

Nehalem
Canoe Races - March
Oregon North Coast International Raft Race - May
Nehalem Arts Festival - July
Nehalem Blackberry Festival - August
Nehalem Music Festival - September

Rockaway Beach
Kite Festival - May
Rockaway Beach Birthday - June
Arts and Crafts Fair - August
Old Fashioned Christmas - November

Garibaldi
Crab Feed and Crab Races - February
Blessing of the Fleet - March
Garibaldi Days - July

Tillamook
Midwinter Festival - March
Dairy Parade and Rodeo - June
Tillamook County Fair - August
Car Club Auto Fun Run - September

Pacific City
Memorial Day Fish Fry - May
Dory Derby Festival - July

Lincoln City
Oregon Wine Festival - April
Senior Craft and Art Show - April
Spring Fling - May
Spring Kite Festival - May
Nelscott Arts and Crafts Fair - June
Sandcastle Building Contest - July
Ocean's Edge 10K Run - July
Flower and Garden Show - August
Children's Festival - August
Dollhouse and Miniature Show - August
Grass Carp Festival - September
International Kite Festival - September
Octoberfest Dinner - October
Driftwood Derby Beach Horserace - October
Artists and Artisans Fair (Gleneden Beach) - October
Christmas Festival and Parade - December

Depoe Bay
Celebration of the Whales - January
Fleet of Flowers Memorial Service - May
Salmon Bake - September

Newport
Seafood and Wine Festival - February
Loyalty Days and Seafair Festival - May
Oregon Coast Gem and Mineral Show - June
Kite Festival - June
Lincoln County Fair and Rodeo - July
Whale Watch Week - December

Waldport
Beachcomber Days - June

Yachats
Arts and Crafts Festival - March

Florence
Annual Beach Clean-up - March
Oregon Dunes Mushers Mill Run - March
Siltcoos Lake Annual Bass Tournament - March
Rhododendron and Azalea Show - March
Rhododendron Festival - Third Weekend in May; includes grand floral parade, carnival, food and crafts fair, chicken barbecue, and a kid's parade
Rhody Downwind Race (sailboarding) - May
Salmon Barbecue - August
Fall Festival - Second Weekend in October; two-day event that includes a clam chowder cook-off, mushroom hunt, dances, entertainment, arts and crafts
Christmas Parade - December

Oregon Dunes National Recreation Area
Migrating flocks of tundra swans - January

Reedsport
Storm Festival - February
Blessing of the Fleet - April
Spring Wine and Dine Festival - May
Sailboard Regatta - June
Ocean Festival - July
Kleo the Crab Contest - September

Coos Bay/North Bend
Governor's Seafood Cook-off - February
Dune Mushers Mail Run - March
Myrtle Tree Festival - March
Youth Festival - May
Whalefest - May
Sandblast in the Dunes - July
North Bend Air Show - July
North Bend Jubilee - July
Oregon Music Festival - July
Blackberry Arts Festival - August
Sand Dune Sashay Square Dance Festival - September
Bay Area Fun Festival - September
Tour de Coast Bicycle Race - September
Prefontaire Memorial 10K Race - September
Oregon Shorebird Festival, Cape Arago Audobon
        Society - September

Charleston
Annual Salmon Barbecue - August

Bandon
Stormwatchers Seafood and Wine Festival - May
Sandcastle Building Contest - May
Fish Fry and Old Time Fiddlers - July
Cranberry Festival - September
Festival of Lights - December

Port Orford
Port Orford Jubilee - July

Gold Beach
Little Reno Night - March
Curry County Fair - September
South Coast Quilt Show - October
Gold Beach Calico Bazaar - November

Brookings
Beachcomber's Festival - March
Azalea Festival - May

BOAT CHARTER AND FISHING GUIDE SERVICES

Astoria
Astoria Cruise and Charter, 325 Industry; 325-0990
Executive Charters, 352 Industry Street; 325-7990
          Evening cruises on Columbia - guide describes area and its history

Hammond
Corkey's Charter Fishing, 1180 Pacific Drive; 861-2668
Columbia Pacific Charter, Hammond Mooring Basin; 861-1527, 861-3303

Warrenton
Warrenton Deep Sea, 45 NE Harbor Place; 861-1233

Nehalem
Jetty Fishery, 27550 Hwy 101, 368-5746; on Nehalem Bay
Wheeler Marina, Wheeler Waterfront; 368-5780

Garibaldi
Siggi-G Charters, 611 Commercial, 322-3285
Troller Garibaldi Deep Sea Fishing, 304 Mooring Basin Rd., 322-3666
Garibaldi Charters, 606 Commercial, 322-0007

Tillamook
Dean's Guide Service, Netarts, 842-7107; drift boat guided fishing on Trask and Wilson Rivers
Rick Howard's Guide Service, 52122 SE Third Place, Scappoose, 543-7372; fishing in Tillamook Bay and river fishing

Pacific City
Tommy Brennan, 32910 State Route 27, Hebo, 392-3019; guided fishing on Nestucca River

Depoe Bay
Allyn's Tradewinds Ocean Sport Fishing, on Hwy. 101 at the north end of the bridge, 765-2345
Dockside Charters, 270 SE Coast Guard Place, next to Coast Guard Station, 800-733-8915
Mostly Fishin'; 765-2954
Deep Sea Trollers, north end of bridge; 765-2248
Depoe Bay Sportfishing, at Jimco; 765-2222
Enterprise Charter & Marine Services; 765-2245

Newport
Fish On Charters, Port Dock 3; 265-8607
Newport Sportfishing, 1000 SE Bay Blvd.; 265-7558
Newport Tradewinds, 653 SW Bay Blvd.; 265-2101
South Beach Charters, at South Beach; 867-7200
Belle of Newport, 345 SW Bay Blvd.; 265-BELL; sternwheeler paddleboat bay cruises
Sea Gull Charters, 343 SW Bay Blvd.; 265-7441

Winchester Bay
Gee Gee Charters Inc., Beach Blvd., at B dock on bay, 271-3152
Terry Jarmain, 1026 Hawthorne, Reedsport, 271-5583; river guided fishing on Umpqua and Smith Rivers
Main Charters, Fourth and Beach Blvd., 271-3800
Ron's River Guide Service, P.O. Box 652, North Bend, 271-4460 or 756-7216
Shamrock Charters, P.O. Box 208, Winchester Bay, 271-3232

Coos Bay Area

Betty Kay Charters, Charleston Boat Basin, 888-9021

Bob's Sportfishing, 7960 Kingfisher Dr., Charleston, 888-4241

Charleston Charters, 5100 Cape Arago Hwy., 888-4846

Don Schrunk, Charleston Boat Basin, 888-2278

Milicoma Guide Service, Coos Bay, 269-0957; guided river fishing services

River Drifter Booking Service, 1333 Bayview Drive, North Bend, 756-6934; books variety of river fishing trips (handicap arrangements)

River Runner Harbor Cruises, Port of Coos Bay City Dock, Anderson Street; bay area and river cruises

Bandon

Coquille River Charters, at boat basin, 347-9093; ocean and river fishing, sightseeing

Dixie Lee Riverboat Trips, 347-3942; sternwheeler trip on Coquille River

Port Orford

Hannah Fishing Lodges, Elk River Road, 332-8585; river fishing on Elk R.

Gold Beach

Rogue Sportfishing Unlimited, Rogue River Reservations, 247-6504; river fishing, jet boat rides

Rogue River Mail Boat Trips, North Bank Rogue Rd., 800-458-3511, 247-7033; jet boat rides (handicapped access)

Jerry's Rogue Jets, south side of bridge, 800-451-3645, 247-4571; jet boat trips

Court's White Water Trips, P.O. Box 1045, Gold Beach, 247-6504

Bill's Fishin' & Jet Boats, 30401 Hillside Terrace; 247-2671; jet boat trips, off-shore fishing

Briggs Charter, 95691 Jerry's Flat Road; 247-7150; ocean and river charters

Greg Eide Guide Service, Box 1248, Gold Beach; 247-2608; river fishing

Rogue River Outfitters, Box 1078, Gold Beach; 247-2684; white water rafting and river fishing

South Coast Guide Service, Jot's Resort; 247-7691

Shamrock Charters, Jot's Resort; 247-6676

McNair Guide Service, Box 1011, Gold Beach; 1-800-451-3645; river fishing

Joe Miller Guide Service, 94771 Indian Creek Road; 247-6772; river fishing

Brookings-Harbor Area

Dick's Sporthaven Marina, 16372 Lower Harbor Rd., Harbor, 469-3301

Leta J Charter, 97748 N. Bank Chetco, Brookings, 469-6964

Lee Myers Guide Service, 15657 Hwy 101 South, 469-6903, drift boat trips on Chetco River

COASTAL MUSEUMS

Museum	Location/Phone	Highlights
Astoria		
Clatsop County Heritage Museum	16th and Duane St. 325-2203	Regional history of Native Americans, fur traders, immigrants, and loggers
Columbia River Maritime Museum	1792 Marine Drive 325-2323	Largest maritime museum in Pacific N.W.; depicts nautical heritage of the Columbia River and North Coast
Fort Clatsop National Memorial	E of Hwy. 101, 5 mi. SE of Astoria 861-2471	Reproduction of Lewis and Clark's winter quarters
Flavel House	441 Eighth Street 325-8395	Home of Capt. George Flavel; exceptional architecture and historical exhibits
Heritage Carter Museum	1618 Exchange 325-8395	Historical artifacts and maritime exhibits
Hammond		
Fort Stevens Historical Museum	Fort Stevens Historical Area 861-2000	Exhibit depicts life of soldier and blacksmith and portrays old fashioned school days; historical fort and batteries
Seaside		
Seaside Museum	570 Necanicum Drive 738-7065	Exhibits of Clatsop Indians, photos, clothing, glassware, and printing equipment
Seaside Aquarium	200 N. Prom 738-6211	Seals, octopus, crabs, fish of every description, and other kinds of marine life
Tillamook		
Tillamook County Pioneer Museum	2106 Second Street 842-4553	Includes natural history, pioneer, and local Native American exhibits; three floors of exhibits containing over 35,000 artifacts and display items
Lincoln City		
Friends of North Lincoln County	1512 SE Hwy. 101 996-6614	Fishing, farming, and logging exhibits; Native American baskets, barn loom, spinning wheel and other artifacts
Lacey's Doll and Antique Museum	3400 NE Hwy 101 994-2392	Antique dishes and furniture; dolls from all over the world

Newport

Name	Address / Phone	Description
Hatfield Marine Science Center	S. Marine Science Dr., south side of Yaquina Bay 867-0100	Exhibits covering the Northwest's marine environment, wildlife exhibits, aquaria, children's tidepool, lectures, wildlife walks and trips
Undersea Gardens	Mariner Square, 250 SW Bay Blvd. 265-2206	Over 5,000 marine specimens visible through windows
Lincoln County Historical Society	545 SW 9th Street 265-7509	Includes Burrows House, displaying glassware, clothing, and household items and a log cabin exhibiting Native American, pioneer, and marine artifacts and early tools
Wax Works Museum	Mariner Square, 250 SW Bay Blvd. 265-2206	Animated wax museum

Yachats

Name	Address / Phone	Description
Little Log Church Museum	Third and Pontiac 547-3976	Features Yachats pioneer artifacts and photos, including original furnishings and a working pump organ

Florence

Name	Address / Phone	Description
Dolly Wares Doll Museum	3620 NW Hwy 101N 997-3391	Display of over 2500 dolls dating from the 1700s to present
Fly-Fishing Museum	280 Nopal 997-6102	Exhibit featuring angling artwork and work of western fly tiers
Siuslaw Pioneer Museum	85294 Hwy. 101S, 1 mi. S of river 997-7884	Indian and pioneer exhibits, early logging equipment

Winchester Bay

Name	Address / Phone	Description
Douglas County Coastal Historical Center	Near lighthouse, 1.5 mi. S of Winchester Bay	Displays of Umpqua River history

North Bend

Name	Address / Phone	Description
Coos County Historical Museum	1220 Sherman Ave., by visitor's center 756-6320	Exhibit features historical and contemporary toys and games; pioneer and Native American artifacts

Coos Bay

Coos Art Museum	235 Anderson Avenue 267-3901	Contemporary art exhibits

Museum	Location/Phone	Highlights
Marshfield-Sun Printing Museum	1049 N. Front St. 269-0215	Historical print shop containing all original newspaper printing presses and equipment
Bandon Coquille River Museum	W. Fir Street, west of old town 347-2164	Native American and marine artifacts, collection of historical photos
Abandoned-by-the-Sea	Big Wheel General Store 347-3587	Possibly the largest collection of driftwood in the world
Myrtle Point Coos County Logging Museum	7th and Maple 572-3153	Historical exhibit featuring logging tools, equipment, and pictures
Gold Beach Curry County Historical Museum	920 S. Ellensburg 247-6113	Exhibit includes historic photos and documents and Native American baskets
Port Orford Hughes House	Cape Blanco State Park 332-2975	1898 house with antiques and photographs
Brookings Chetco Valley Historical Society Museum	15461 Museum Road 469-6651	Home of pioneer family, featuring antique furniture, photographs, gold-mining equipment

BIBLIOGRAPHY

Alt, D.D. and D.W. Hyndman. 1989. Roadside Geology of Oregon. Mountain Press Publishing Co., Missoula, MT.

Barnhart, D. and V. Lion. 1989. Tidepools. Blake Publishing Co., San Luis Obispo, CA.

Blood, Marge. 1986. Exploring the Oregon Coast By Car. Image Imprints, Eugene, OR.

Canniff, K. 1988. A Camper's Guide to Oregon and Washington. Ki² Enterprises, Portland, Oregon.

Casali, D. and M. Diness. 1988. Fishing in Oregon. Flying Pencil Publications, Portland, OR.

Evanich, J.E., Jr. 1990. The Birder's Guide to Oregon. Portland Audubon Society, Portland, OR.

Faubion, W. 1986. You are Invited to the Best Choices on the Oregon Coast. Apple Press Publishing, Portland, OR.

Goodnight, J. and S. Vickerman. 1987. Oregon Wildlife Viewing Guide. Defenders of Wildlife, Lake Oswego, OR.

Johnson, J.A. 1990. Clamming and Crabbing in Oregon. Adventure North Publishing Co., Gardiner, OR.

Jones, S. 1972. Oregon Saltwater Fishing Guide. Stan Jones Publishing, Inc., Seattle, WA.

Kirkendall, T. and V. Spring. 1984. Bicycling the Pacific Coast. The Mountaineers, Seattle, WA.

Kozloff, E.N. 1983. Seashore life of the Northern Pacific Coast. An Illustrated Guide to Northern California, Oregon, Washington, and British Columbia. University of Washington Press, Seattle, WA.

Lilja, I. and D. Lilja. 1990. Siuslaw Forest Hikes. A Guide to Oregon's Central Coast Range Trails. Heritage Associates, Inc., Albuquerque, NM.

Mainwaring, W.L. 1977. Exploring the Oregon Coast. Westridge Press, Salem, OR.

McConnaughey, B.H. and E. McConnaughey. 1988. Pacific Coast. Audobon Society Nature Guide. Chanticleer Press, New York, NY.

McCrae, J. and L. Osis. 1989. Plants and Animals of Oregon's Rocky Intertidal Habitat. Oregon Department of Fish and Wildlife, Newport, OR.

Oberrecht, K. 1990. Driving the Pacific Coast. Oregon and Washington. The Globe Pequot Press, Chester, CT.

Olmsted, G.W. 1989. The Best of the Pacific Coast. San Francisco to British Columbia. Crown Publishers, New York, NY.

Ostertag, R. and G. Ostertag. 1989. 50 Hikes in Oregon's Coast Range and Siskiyous. The Mountaineers, Seattle, WA.

Ramsey, F.L. 1978. Birding Oregon. Audubon Society, Corvallis, OR.

Remington, J.D. 1987. Mountain Bike Guide to Oregon. Oregon State Department of Parks and Recreation. Salem, Oregon.

Ross, C.R. 1989. Trees to know in Oregon. Oregon State University, Corvallis, Oregon.

Shelley, J. 1990. Golf courses of the Pacific Northwest. Alaska Northwest Books, Anchorage, Alaska.

Snively, G. 1978. Exploring the Seashore in British Columbia, Washington, and Oregon. A Guide to Shorebirds and Intertidal Plants and Animals. Gordon Soules Book Publishers, Vancouver, B.C.

Spring, B. and I. Spring. 1978. Oregon Wildlife Areas. Superior Publ. Co., Seattle, WA.

Sullivan, W.L. 1988. Exploring Oregon's Wild Areas. The Mountaineers, Seattle, WA.

West, V.C. 1984. A Guide to Shipwreck Sites Along the Oregon Coast. R.E. Wells and V.C. West Publishers, North Bend, OR.

Williams, P.M. 1985. Oregon Coast Hikes. The Mountaineers, Seattle, WA.

Index

Gazetteer

The gazetteer is an alphabetical listing of names which refer to places located on the Oregon coast. Following each name is found the number of the sectional map(s) on which the place is depicted. Sectional maps are numbered 1-24, proceeding north to south.

Agate Beach, **10**
Alsea Bay, **11**
Astoria, **1**
Bandon, **18**
Bandon Marsh National Wildlife Refuge, **18**
Barview, **5**
Bayocean, **5**
Beachside State Park, **11**
Beverly Beach State Park, **9**
Blimp Hangers, **5**
Bob Straub State Park, **7**
Boiler Bay, **9**
Bradley Lake, **18**
Brookings, **24**
Bullards Beach State Park, **18**
Cannon Beach, **3**
Cape Arago, **17**
Cape Arago Lighthouse, **17**
Cape Arago State Park, **17**
Cape Blanco, **20**
Cape Blanco Light, **20**
Cape Blanco State Park, **20**
Cape Falcon, **3**
Cape Ferello, **24**
Cape Foulweather, **9**
Cape Kiwanda, **6**
Cape Kiwanda State Park, **6**
Cape Lookout, **6**
Cape Lookout State Park, **5,6**
Cape Meares, **5**
Cape Meares State Park, **5**
Cape Perpetua, **12**
Cape Sebastian, **23**
Carl Washburne State Park, **12**
Cascade Head, **7**
Charleston, **17**
Chetco River, **24**
Clatsop Spit, **1**
Clear Lake, **15**
Cleawox Lake, **14**
Coffenbury Lake, **1**
Columbia River, **1**
Coos Bay, **16,17**
Coquille River, **18**
Coquille River Lighthouse, **18**
Curry County Historical Museum, **22**
D River, **8**

Darlingtonia Botanical Gardens, **13**
Depoe Bay, **9**
Devil's Churn, **12**
Devil's Elbow, **12**
Devil's Punchbowl, **9**
Devils Lake, **8**
Drift Creek, **8**
Ecola State Park, **2,3**
Eel Lake, **15**
Elk River, **20**
Face Rock, **18**
Floras Lake, **19,20**
Florence, **13**
Fogarty Creek, **9**
Fort Stevens, **1**
Fort Stevens State Park, **1**
Garibaldi, **5**
Garrison Lake, **20**
Gearhart, **2**
Gleneden Beach, **8**
Goat Island, **24**
Gold Beach, **22**
Governor Patterson State Park, **11**
Grisel Monument State Park, **22**
Harbor, **24**
Harris Beach State Park, **24**
Hatfield Marine Science Center, **10**
Haystack Rock, **3,6**
Heceta Head, **12**
Horsfall Lake, **16**
Hughes House, **20**
Humbug Mountain, **21**
Humbug Mountain State Park, **21**
Jesse Honeyman State Park, **14**
Kilchis River, **5**
Lakeside, **15**
Langlois, **19**
Lincoln City, **8**
Little Nestucca River, **7**
Manzanita, **4**
Miami River, **5**
Neahkannie Mountain, **4**
Nehalem, **4**
Nehalem Bay, **4**
Nehalem Bay State Park, **4**
Neptune State Park, **12**
Nesika Beach, **22**
Neskowin, **7**

About the Author

Timothy Sullivan's interest and involvement in outdoor recreation is of long standing. His educational background includes a Bachelor's degree in liberal arts from Stonehill College in Massachusetts, Master's in biology from Western State College of Colorado, and Ph.D. in biological sciences from Oregon State University. He has worked as a back-country ranger in a primitive area in the Colorado mountains, conducted acid rain research for two years in Norway, and taught college and community college courses in natural history, ornithology, and wildlife biology. Dr. Sullivan is currently president and principal scientist for E&S Environmental Chemistry, Inc., an environmental research firm that specializes in water quality, air quality, and environmental assessment. He has authored over 30 publications on environmental topics. An Oregon resident since 1978, he spends considerable time at the Oregon coast with his wife and two children.

About the Cartographers

Joseph Bernert is a geographer with E&S Geographic and Information Services. His educational background includes a Master's degree in Geography from Oregon State University. He has directed the cartographic and geographic components of numerous natural resource studies at E&S, and is highly experienced in geographic information systems (GIS) and computer systems design. Born and raised in Oregon, he is an avid outdoor recreationist who enjoys backpacking, bicycling, white water rafting, and fishing.

Sharon Murfield-Tyler is a geographical assistant and cartographer with E&S and is completing a Master's degree in geography at Oregon State University. She has experience in GIS and computer-aided map creation and design. Originally from South Dakota, she moved to Oregon in 1989 with her husband, Dean, and three children, and enjoys hiking, camping, travel, and photography.

****

ORDER FORM

To order the **Oregon Coast Recreational Atlas**, please send check or money order for $11.95 per copy, plus shipping costs, to:

E&S Geographic and Information Services
Department OC-21
P.O. Box 609
Corvallis, OR 97339

Telephone (503) 758-6305
FAX: (503) 758-7319

Number of copies ___ x $11.95 =	_____
Shipping (see below)	_____
Total Enclosed	_____

Name _____

Address _____

City _____ State _____ Zip _____

Shipping

Book Rate: $1.75 for the first book and 75 cents for each additional book (allow 3 to 4 weeks)

First Class: $3.00 per book